A How-to Book for Hard Times

Gillian Kirkpatrick

iUniverse, Inc.
New York   Bloomington

A How-to Book for Hard Times

iUniverse books may be ordered through booksellers or by contacting:
iUniverse

1663 Liberty Drive
Bloomington, IN 47403
www.iuniverse.com
1-800-Authors (1-800-288-4677)

Because of the dynamic nature of the Internet, any Web addresses or links contained in this book may have changed since publication and may no longer be valid. The views expressed in this work are solely those of the author and do not necessarily reflect the views of the publisher, and the publisher hereby disclaims any responsibility for them.

ISBN: 978-1-4401-3609-2 (sc)
ISBN: 978-1-4401-3610-8 (e-book)

Printed in the United States of America
iUniverse rev. date: 4/29/2009

CONTENTS

A How-to Book for Hard Times.

Another 'How-to Book', why? Well hard times come in many different ways, and hopefully, this little book can help with some of them. I've drawn on experience from myself and others. From World War 2, depression, to to many kids and to little money, out of work and just getting started. Living in a foreign land without knowledge of the language. I hope in pooling all this into a book it can help someone have an easier time in hard times, maybe even a little laughter. Laughter always makes the day a little brighter. That's what I hope to do with knowledge from the past to make the future brighter. Anyhow, that's why this How-to Book.

CHAPTER 1

*How to make and follow
a menu guide*

How to make and
follow a menu guide.

Now to really get started. What to do first? Well what comes to my mind is how to feed my family? You need to know how to make and follow a menu guide.

Notice I said guide, that means you don't have to make what's down for that day on that day, it's just a guide for that week or month.

To do this you will need a calendar with nice big daily squares. Make one or buy one it really doesn't matter. Plan your menu according to how often you get paid: weekly, biweekly, or monthly. Then sit down and figure out breakfast, lunch, dinner and snacks. Figure out what you need to make those meals and make a shopping list of all you need to buy to make those meals.

NEVER go shopping when you are hungry, it can really hurt your budget. Try to buy a little extra of the things you use most often, this will start you on your storage to stockpile for your needs. Remember you don't have to cook what the menu says on that day, but cross out the meals as you make them, that way you know what's left to make.

As you go along try to have meals from your stock, this way your body gets used to them, and will also help you rotate your supplies.

CHAPTER 2

Stocking up on basic supplies

Stocking up on basic supplies

You'll need to start stocking up on basic supplies. You don't have to get them all at once, just a little at a time. So I'll give you a list of very basic food needs figured out for one adult, cut in half ,or less, for toddlers but double for teens.Teen years need more nutrition.

The list I will give you should cover an amount for 1 month. Get it slowly, store it but keep it in rotation by using it in your menus. So put supplies in good storage containers, and always mark with month and year. Always put new to the back of shelves and pull the old forward for easy use. Remember this is only for a month, you need to build that up to a year or so. Do it slowly so that it wont be hard on your budget.

> Grains [wheat, rice, corn or other cereal.]
> 25lbs. Per person.
> Nonfat dry milk 6 1/4lbs. Per person.
> Sugar or honey 5lbs. Per person.
> Salt 7oz. Per person.
> Fat or oil 1lb.10oz. Per person.
> Dried Legumes , 5lbs per
> person.

For those people who have diabetes use sugar and salt substitutes in equal amounts. The same applies to others with medical problems, don't neglect to store your substitutes.

Please remember to keep things in rotation, this will keep your storage fresh, so use it often. Don't buy things you wont eat. When times are hard one doesn't take well to new and untried tastes, what we're used to and comfortable with works best.

Be sure to store a variety of foods, those that are readily available and not to costly.

To go along with your supply of wheat , or other grains, you will need a wheat grinder or mill. Metal grinders are easier to use. Best to buy a manual one in case of power failure. When grinding wheat, for flour only, grind enough for what you need then.

Whole wheat does not store well. When you buy wheat for storing buy dark hard winter or dark hard spring wheat. Buy #2 grade. Make sure it is clean and has no insects. Store in a sturdy, moisture proof container. Metal containers with tight lids are best.

Enriched grains are really important they contain vitamin B, magnesium, iron and fiber. Avoid storing any grain in an open container. Store in a clean, cool, dry place , off the floor. Rotate the supply.

Powdered milk. Buy only "extra" grade dry milk should be stored in a tightly covered container [metal, rigid plastic, or glass] and stored in a cool, dry, dark location up off the floor. To help you rotate powdered milk here are some tips. Mix a quart of milk made from powder with a quart of whole milk and refrigerate overnight. That's for drinking. Use just powdered for cooking. To make powdered milk taste better add vanilla, honey, cream or canned milk, always serve it after refrigerating overnight.

Canned milk, it has a shelf life of 1 to 2 years. Powdered baby formula has a shelf life of 2 years. Non dairy creamers shelf life is 1 to 4 years, if vacuum packed.

Cheese spread & Powdered cheese, spread has a shelf life of 1 year and powdered has an average shelf life of 15 years.

Sugar and or Honey. This is really important in storage. When times are hard something sweet seems to help things not to seem to be so bad, especially for children. So make sure you have sweet makings in your storage, you'll be really glad you do.

White Sugar, if stored in a cool dry place in a sealed container, will keep indefinitely.

Brown Sugar needs to be kept moist, a piece of apple does the trick. Keep in containers with tight fitting lids. Brown Sugar and Powdered Sugar have a shelf life of 3 years.

Corn Syrup may crystallize after long storing, put the container in a pan of hot water and the crystals will melt. Corn Syrup has a shelf life of 5 years.

Honey, in crystalline form, no water, stored at room temperature, will last indefinitely. This type of honey has 400 less calories than a pound of sugar. The greatest amount of honey is sold in liquid form. This type of honey has a shelf life of 3 years. You can also get creamed honey, this is easier to spread, no drips. Keep in the fridge if temps are to warm. Honey can be used measure for measure in place of sugar. The Honey Association recommends that infants under 1 year should not be given honey, because it is a raw product and may contain bacteria.

Jams and Preserves have a shelf life of 4 years.

Jell-O and Pudding mix packages have a shelf life of 3 years.

Powdered drink mixes & Syrups last for 5years.

Carmel, in a box, lasts for 1 year ,if coated for 2 years.

Hard candy, in a can, lasts for 5 years.

Jellied candy, in a box, lasts for 2 years. This will help keep children happy, also a treat for good deeds.

Salt is necessary, unless a medical condition prohibits,the best form is iodized salt. Both iodized table salt and salt substitute keep indefinitely. In hot climates you need more than the recommended amount.Also allow extra in your storage to cover the use of salt in pickling. You may want to have some rock salt for making ice cream. The body needs about 1 ½ tsps of salt daily.

Fat and or oil supply energy and are a source of vitamins A, D, E, and K. Olive oil, in a can, has a shelf life of 1 ½ years.

Margarine, in a can, is good for 5 years. **Mayonnaise** is good for 10 months.

Lard, in a carton, is good for 1 year.

Peanut Butter, do make sure to have this, as it's a really good source of protein, and most children love it. Peanut Butter is good for 5 years.

Salad oil, in a can, has a shelf life of 2 years.

Salad dressing is only good for 8 months. **Shortening**, in a can, has a shelf life of 5 years.

Butter, wrapped and refrigerated, has a shelf life of a few months.

Legumes and Nuts. Beans are a good source of protein and can be a substitute for meat. Dried beans, properly stored, have a shelf life of many years. They should be kept in tightly covered metal, plastic or glass containers. Keep them in a dark, dry and cool place. Older beans will require longer soaking when being used. Soybeans can be sprouted for a salad or served as a veggie.

T.V.P. ,textured vegetable protein, is made from soybeans, its texture is similar to meat. TVP comes in meat flavors, beef, ham, bacon or chicken. It has a shelf life of 2 to 3 years.

Nuts are also a good source of protein. Whole nuts keep best for long storage. Pour them into a strong mesh bag and hang in a cool dry place, or put them in a perforated container, this allows the air to circulate around them. This way they should keep for at least 8 months.

WATER. We are blessed that we can buy water in easily stored bottles. Do remember, it's so very important, ROTATE. It is recommended we drink 6 to 8 glasses a day, and that's just drinking water. Water is needed for cooking, washing oneself and cleaning. So how to do this? Well the drinking and cooking water is easy, bottles store in a cool place up off the floor. That only needs to be a couple of inches off the floor.Keep them in rotation. A good way to have water for cleaning etc. is to have rain barrels to collect rain water. In case of disasters it is always good to have iodine pills for water purification. They have a shelf life of 3 to 5 years, please follow directions on the bottle. This way you can make sure your water is not contaminated.

Vitamins. Make sure to have the appropriate ones for each member of the family. Be aware of the expiration date and keep them rotated.

Coffee kept in an air tight container squeeze as much air as possible out and store in a cool dry place it will keep indefinitely. Freezing an unopened bag of coffee beans is the best way to store them. Best flavor is only 2 weeks after opening the bag.

Tea, regular and Herbal, kept in an air tight container and store in a cool dry place it will keep indefinitely

Cocoa in a carton kept in an air tight container and store in a cool dry place it will last for 3 yrs, in a can for 5yrs.

MREs, meals ready to eat. This is the U.S. military's current field ration for all ground troops. Stored in a dry location they will keep for 7 to 10 years. To keep best quality they should be rotated every 6 years. Since they are fully cooked they can be eaten heated or cold. When storing them do not expose them to high heat nor freeze them. Now that we have covered the very basics we need to make this supply tastier. A lot depends on your family's likes and dislikes. So I thought I'd give you a list of foods and their shelf life to help you build your storage up. This information is to help you keep things in rotation. Please date all items and keep a list of your storage.

Apples ,canned .6 yrs.

Apple Butter ,4 yrs.

Apple, baby food .,3 yrs.

Apple, dehydrated, can. 3 yrs.

Apple juice ,can. 5 yrs.

Asparagus, can .5 yrs.

Bacon, can .4 yrs.

Bakery ,mixes, 1 yr.

Baking Powder ,can. 2 yrs.

Beef, Liver, Pork or Veal baby foods, jar. 2 ½ yrs.

Beef, corned, can. 5 yrs.

Beets, baby food,. jar .2 yrs.

Beets, regular can .3 yrs.

Catsup ,bottle. 4 yrs.

Cereal, ready to eat. 2 yrs.

Cereal, quick cook. 1yr.

Cereal, sugar coated .1yr

Chewing gum ,9 mths.

Chicken ,can. 5 yrs.

Chicken, baby food, jar .2 ½ yrs.

Clams, can. 4 yrs.

Cookies, carton .6 mths

Cornmeal ,package. 3 yrs.

Crackers, Graham .4 mths

Crackers, oyster, soda .6 mths.

Cranberry sauce ,can .4 yrs.

Cream, coffee type. 1 yr.

Creamer, substitute .5 yrs.

Currants ,dried .2yrs

Eggs, dehydrated ,can. 5 yrs.

Flour ,bag ,better stored in a container. 2 yrs.

Fruit Cocktail ,can. 4 yrs.

Fry mix breading, bag, 2 yrs.

Grape juice ,can ,5 yrs.

Ham chunks ,can ,5 yrs.

Hominy, grits, 3 yrs

Luncheon meat ,can ,5 yrs.

Macaroni ,carton, 4 yrs.

Mustard ,jar, 3 yrs

Mushroom ,can ,4 ½ yrs.

Noodles, egg, carton. 3 yrs.

Olives, green, jar, 3yrs

Onion, dehydrated ,can .4 yrs.

Salmon ,can, 5 yrs.

Sauces, hot, kitchen, meat, soy or Worcestershire, bottle, 4 yrs.

Sardines, can ,4 yrs.

Sardines in tomato sauce, can ,2 yrs.

Shortening ,can ,5 yrs.

Shrimp, can ,4 yrs.

Soups, ready to serve ,can, 4 yrs.

Spaghetti, carton, 4 yrs.

Spices, seasonings, or Herbs ,can .5yrs ,

Container. 3yrs.

Tuna, water pack ,can ,4 yrs.

Tuna, oil pack, can ,5 yrs.

Yeast, bakers active, dry ,can ,6 mths.

Popcorn, unopened ,can/jar, 6 yrs.

Popcorn ,carton ,2 mths.

Raisins ,can, 3 yrs.

Meat, dehydrated ,can ,5 yrs.

Want a goodie that will last for ever? I've heard that Twinkies fit the bill.

For your Pets. If you have pets you will need to have their needs in your storage. Dry food stores well, it's also good to have some canned food on hand, check expiration dates and keep rotated. For cats, if they are indoor ones , you will need kitty litter, add a little baking soda to keep fresh longer. If you have fish don't forget the aquarium needs. Also their food. Birds will need their seed . Other small pets will need their food and bedding supplies. If you have chickens or turkeys don't forget their food. It wouldn't hurt to have vitamins for each pet. Pets can be very important as they bring a lot of happiness in hard times, so take care of them and their needs to keep them healthy.

Babies. We must also take care of the special needs of babies. Make sure your storage has diapers. Disposables 8 to 12 a day. Cloth diapers you'll need 6 dozen, if you combine with disposable you will need 3 dozen cloth ones and 6 disposable a day. Make sure you have large safety pins, baby wipes, baby lotion, baby shampoo and soap. Ear drops in case of ear infections. Warm olive oil can also help with ear infections, put a little bit of cotton in the ear after putting the oil in to keep the oil in the ear. Make sure you have liquid baby vitamins, strained baby food, baby bottles, pacifier and teething ring. For toddlers a good finger food is graham crackers. They have a shelf life of about a year if you keep them in a metal container. Make sure you have all the baby and toddler clothing you need, good to shop thrift stores for these.

CHAPTER 3

Preserving Food

Preserving food

Veggies There are various ways of preserving them. The easiest is freezing. For your root veggies a root cellar is good. You can also use your basement. Where ever you decide to store your fresh produce it must be well ventilated and cool. Even if you don't have land there are other ways to grow some veggies. For small plots of land raised beds make better use of the space. Stepped boxes is another idea. Narrow boxes with a trellis are also good ideas. Growing in containers is a good idea for anywhere, indoors or outdoors. Window boxes are also a good place to grow things. So even if you live in a city container gardening will give you some fresh herbs and veggies

Freezing is a very easy way to preserve food. You do need some equipment to do this. For the foods you can preserve raw all you will need are good freezer bags. I always double bag. After getting all the air I can out of the main bag. This way I don't get freezer burn on the food so easily. Don't forget to date your bags. Always use oldest first. Some foods you will need to par cook or blanche. You need 2 large pans for this, one for blanching or steaming , the other for cold water to cool the food down fast before freezing. Divide the food into small amounts, enough for 2 to 3 people, smaller amounts freeze better. For foods that are to delicate for bags, berries, there are very good freezer containers. Try to get fresh fruit and produce into freezer within 2 hours of harvesting, this will give you the best flavor. In case your freezer is without electricity, for what ever reason, try to get some dry ice and put it in your freezer. Food will keep in your freezer, without dry ice, for about 2 days, if you don't open the door to often. Don't skimp on your wrappings and containers that you use for freezing. Better or more will preserve your food in the best shape. Don't forget to date all items.

Canning is probably the most practical way to preserve food. You will need a good canning book , to give you good instructions on how to process different foods. Either Ball Blue Book Home Canning Manual, or Kerr Home Canning Manual. You will need a boiling water bath canner. It should be deep enough to cover, by 2 inches, your canning jars. Buy a good brand of canning jars and lids. The jars will be reusable for many years. However you will need a supply of lids and rings as they are not reusable. You may also want a pressure canner. Pressure canning is really needed for meats, sauces,and low acid foods.. For any canning you will also need a jar funnel, jar lifter, helps not to burn fingers, and a plastic spatula. A lid wand helps you get lids out of boiling water. You will also need labels to date your finished product. Your finished product can be kept in the boxes the jars came in, if you do this label and date the outside of the box.

Drying or dehydrating. This is one of the oldest methods of food preservation. It doesn't require a lot of equipment. Food can be dried in the sun, in the oven, in a microwave or in a dehydrator. Good fruits to dry are apples, peaches, apricots, pears, plums, cherries, figs, grapes, berries but not strawberries. A fruit treat that is expensive to buy can be easily made it is fruit leather. Fruit leather is made by drying fruit pulp into a thin sheet and then rolling it up for storage. Any type of fruit can be used, the only ones not suitable for it are grapefruit, lemons, persimmons and rhubarb. Dehydrated food stores well. Suitable containers for storage include glass jars, metal cans with tightly fitting lids and plastic containers. Again make sure to date and rotate. Because in dehydrating moisture has been removed allow the extra water to hydrate them in your storage. Boiling water shortens the rehydration time. Don't add sugar or salt till the final 5 minutes.

Smoking and curing. Smoking is a simple method of drying out the meat. Smoked meat needs no refrigeration. If electricity goes off for a long time, meats in the freezer could be thawed and smoked. Most types of meat and fish can be smoked. Types of smokers include a small building, a wooden barrel and portable smokers.

STORING FRESH VEGGIES.

Artichokes, Asparagus, Beans, Broccoli, Collards, Eggplant, Endive, Kale, Lettuce, Mushrooms, Mustard greens, Okra, Peas, Radishes, Spinach, Sweet corn and Swiss chard. Refrigerate and use with in 8 days.

Beets, Brussels sprouts, Cauliflower, Celery, Leeks, Melons, Onions, Radicchio and Summer squash. Can refrigerate up to 12 weeks.
Cabbage, Carrots, Kohlrabi, Parsnips, Potatoes, Rutabagas and Turnips. Can be kept if cool and damp for 18 weeks.

Garlic and Onions, not green onions
can keep if cool and dry for 7 months.
Pumpkin and Winter Squash. if kept warm and dry will keep for 2 to 3 months.

CHAPTER 4

Things you need to have

Things you need to have

Next is a list of things you need to have, and you may already have, around the house to help keep things running smoothly. For small repairs you'll need a hammer, nails, straight edge and Philips screwdrivers and screws. A handsaw that you can handle, pliers, needle nose pliers are handy for working with small things, vise grips, metal and rubber washers, wrench, hand or electric drill, axe, hatchet, pick, shovel and small ladder. If you have yard space for growing veggies make sure you have a spade, hoe, rake, lawn mower, watering can and or hoses. After thought be good to have extra fuses. One needs to have a supply of candles for light in case of a storm or electrical outage. Would be good to have a flashlight in each room. A supply of batteries, flashlight bulbs, the brightest ones are krypton or halogen. Be nice to have a battery operated radio. It's good to know what's going on during a blackout and why. You can get hand crank radios at a reasonable price. Kerosene and or oil lamps are a good source of light. Don't forget the fuel to keep them going. If you choose lamps for lighting don't forget wicks or mantels will be needed, keep extras in your storage. A camping stove, in case of prolonged black outs, and appropriate fuel is good to have, just in case. And oh yes, lots of stick matches and lighters, and fuel, good for lighting candles, lamps, stoves and maybe a fireplace if you are so blessed. Make sure you have extra light bulbs and fuses too. Have a good supply of toilet paper, good for blowing noses as well as toilet use. Make sure you have Clorox, good for so many things, white vinegar is a good cleaner, ammonia is also a good cleaning agent, baking soda, liquid detergent.

Your own personal feminine needs, shampoo and lotion. For men hand razors, razor blades, shaving cream and after shave. Tooth paste and tooth brushes for each member of the family. Body deodorants for all. If you or someone in your family has dentures make sure you have denture cream and cleaner in stock. You might also think about having a carpet sweeper, good when electricity is out. Mineral oil and Vaseline are good to have on hand.

CHAPTER 5

First aid supplies

First aid supplies

If you have little ones lots of band aids, Neosporin & rubbing alcohol. To clean cuts and scrapes betadine is a good antiseptic.

Bandages, ace bandage and a cloth sling.

If you have a baby zinc oxide ointment is really good for diaper rash and destine is also good for diaper rash.

Calamine lotion or Caladryl lotion are good for soothing bites, poison ivy, poison sumac and poison oak.

Corn starch is good for heat rash.

Benedryl is good for allergies.

Laxatives to relieve constipation, prunes are good for this.

Cough medicines and cough drops to help with chest congestion and decongestants to help with stuffy noses.

Diarrhea medicine.

Aspirin or equilivent.

CHAPTER 6

Clothes and mending supplies

Clothes and mending supplies

Now we need to think of clothes and mending supplies. Always watch end of season sales. If you have little ones this is a good time to buy for the following year. Buy clothes 1 or 2 sizes bigger than what they are now wearing. Buy in plain colors, easy to match or decorate. You can do the same with shoes. For adults and teens it's also good to shop the seasonal sales. If you can sew you need to watch the fabric store sales. Cotton, flannel and muslin are sturdy fabrics. Also corduroy, denim and perma press fabrics. Firmly woven fabrics wear longer than light weight ones. Dark colored clothing, also prints and plaids, look nice longer, not showing soil and wear so quickly. Also watch for pattern sales. Get simple patterns that can be easily adjusted. A few words on clothing; make sure everyone has a warm winter coat, rain gear, thick socks, thermal underwear, mittens or gloves and a warm winter hat. You can also check out your local thrift stores for these items. Along with clothing don't forget bedding, sleeping bags and extra pillows. Again watch for sales and thrift stores can be a good place to get quilts, blankets, sheets, towels and washcloths.

Mending and sewing. For mending and sewing you will need scissors, needles of all sizes, pins and a pin cushion, safety pins, seam ripper, masking tape, threads in the most often used colors, snaps, zippers, hooks and eyes, elastic, an assortment of buttons, thimble, tape measure, darning bulb or use a light bulb carefully and darning yarn. If you are going to actually make clothes make sure you have a good basic sewing machine and stock up on supplies for it. You will need sewing machine needles, sewing machine oil, and bobbins.

Keeping clothing in good repair. for socks, you'll need to know how to darn. Darning is like weaving, but first you must go around the edge of the hole, that needs repairing, with a simple running stitch, not to close to the edge or the darn wont hold. Then go from one side to the opposite side, not to tightly, till the hole is filled in. Then go in the opposite direction, only take your needle and thread and go under the first thread, then over the next one do this till one row is done, catch the fabric at the end of the row and turn to do the next row. Do this till you have completely filled in the hole. Completed it will look like a basket weave or making a pot holder. End your darning with a back stitch so that it wont come undone. You can mend all kinds of clothing this way if you don't have patching material. It's good to have odds and ends of material on hand, especially if you have children. As children grow out of their clothing save what you can for patching and making quilts.

Quilting is a fun way for little ones to learn basic sewing. Turning hems around the edges of squares or other shapes, then helping to sew squares together before starting to tie up the quilt. Quilting can be a fun project for all of the family.

If you know how to knit or crochet make sure you have a supply of yarn. Watch for sales on yarn, patterns, needles and hooks. This is a good way to have nice fitting warm sweaters, socks, hats, gloves and afghans.

To take care of shoes and boots make sure to have shoe polish, extra laces and inner soles.

CHAPTER 7

*Making the most of
your family's time*

Making the most of your family's time.

 In writing this list I remembered a time when my family and I had a blackout for several days. I was so glad we were together and had good supplies. My children were excited, after the first scare of no electricity. We got out oil lamps and camping lanterns, they're good to read by. We always had a good supply of board games. They're so much fun and draw family's together. Our favorites were Monopoly,Sorry and Clue. Then there are always good card games, Fish, Old Maid, Snap and War. We also liked Uno. Along with some snacks, popcorn and popcorn balls, no one was scared and a good family time was had by all. During daylight hours there's lots of fun to be had, after chores, playing lots of games. Hide and seek is good indoors or out side. Tag and Blind mans bluff. Blind mans bluff is played with one person being blind folded, turned around 3 times then tries to find someone and guess who they are. If they can't guess they get turned around again and try again. When they finally guess correctly that person takes their place. Start all over again. Jump rope is an outdoor pleasure and really good exercise. If you have a flat piece of concrete or sidewalk Hop Scotch is a really good game.

These are just a few ideas for outdoor games for family fun. A really fun game for all ages is charades. Twister is good indoors or outdoors, kids really love it.

My most favorite thing has always been to read a good book, also good indoors or outdoors. Even during the blackouts of World War 2, I would get a flashlight, torch in England, my book and make a tent out of my blankets and there safely escaped the sound of air raids. I could enter into the land of my books. So reading is a great pleasure.

Moms and Dads can read to their little ones till they can learn to read for themselves. I've only mentioned a few simple forms of entertainment. They're all family oriented; in hard times, families need to pull together, have fun, and make working together a pleasure. Then times won't feel nearly as hard.

Sitting down with your family and talking is one of the best things to do in troubled times. Together decide what you need to do, who or what you can trust. That's an interesting question with a really great answer. Look around, who created all things, was it not God? He is the one you can trust, rely on His guidance for little or big things, you can trust Him. It's because of His love for us that all these things are here for our use. He has provided so much for our use, and hopefully this book can help you see how to use the things available to us all.

CHAPTER 8

Keeping up you home and vehicles.

Keeping up you home and vehicles.

Taking care of the basic needs of a car. You'll need to keep the fluids and anti-freeze on hand. Your owners manual will have a list of other needs. If you don't have the manual go to the library and look it up.

For small repairs around the home you'll need some other items as well as the tools I listed. Some wood, 1"x2", 2"x4", partial sheets of plywood or particle board.. Wood glue and wood putty are good to have on hand. Masking tape and Duct tape are really important to have. You wouldn't believe what I have repaired with Duct tape, much to my sons disgust. Hey, it worked, isn't that what matters?

CHAPTER 9

Herbs

HERBS.

So lets begin with herbs. You need to know I'm not a wonderful chef, so bare with me please. I've had no training in the culinary arts. I got married very young and learned from watching friends cook. Some of these herbs I'd never seen or heard of, but friends told me they were good; I researched them and I've included them. I do know herbs make the food taste good and they're good for you. Lots of vitamins and soothing to the tummy.

ANGELICA: grows in zones 4-9. It is a biennial, every other year. Angelica grows from 5 to 8 feet tall. The flowers are great rounded, Queen Ann's Lace like, umbels up to 10" in diameter. They consist of many small green honey scented flowers. They bloom in June or July in the 2nd or 3rd year of growth. They have broad leaves with toothed edges. Plants die back in the winter. Angelica likes a moderately moist, slightly acid , soil.Prefers partial shade but will grow in full shade, if mulched will grow in sun. Sow seeds do not cover as they need light to germinate. Collect seeds in late summer. Enclose whole seed heads when nearly ripe. If not growing for seeds remove flowers early to prolong life of plant. Store when thoroughly dry, or they mold, in an air tight container in the fridge. They can be kept for up to 1yr. Angelica seeds are used in cooking cakes and beverages, chop stems to sweeten deserts. For best quality gather leaves and stems in morning after dew has dried, in spring and summer before plant flowers. **Do Not Gather in the wild as there is a Poisonous look alike.**

ANISE: is an annual self seeding plant. It grows 2 feet tall and 1 to 2 feet wide. Whitish umbel, Queen Ann's lace like, flowers bloom in summer. Anises ferny leaves resemble Queen Ann's Lace. Anise has a spicy sweet, licorice-like flavor and aroma. You can substitute Anise seeds for Caraway seeds in breads and crackers. Add to bouillon or fish stock. Use fresh leaves and seeds in salad. Also use leaves with chicken, fish and veggies. Anise aids digestion. Use a strong infusion, a tea,of leaves to ease a cough. Also supposed to help with flatulence, gas. Sow seeds in spring, can be started indoors in peat or newspaper pots. Transplant when damage from frost is over. Plant in full sun. Grows best in light, lean, well drained soil. **Do Not Fertilize.** Plant 1 foot apart, plant in groups of 5 or stake single plants. These plants are pest and disease free. Pick leaves in summer before plants bloom. Collect seeds in early fall. When seeds are ripe, cut whole seed heads, anytime after dew has dried. Enclose seed heads to prevent droppings. Let seeds dry fully, then store in tightly covered jars. Strip leaves, from cut stems, in morning for drying. Anise is an excellent companion plant for cilantro.

ANISE HYSSOP: is a perennial plant that will grow in zones 5-9. Anise Hyssop grows to 3 feet tall. Flowers are spikes of lavender and bloom from summer to fall. It has mint-like leaves with toothed edges. Plant dies back in winter. Anise Hyssop smells and tastes like "green" licorice. This is an ornamental herb. Tasty as well as pretty, it is useful in teas, salads, and cooking. Looks pretty in the garden as well as in flower arrangements. Fresh leaves are good in salads, also dried for teas. The licorice flavor compliments some fish and chicken dishes. A strong tea aids digestion.Plant Anise Hyssop a week before last frost, or start in peat, or newspaper pots, 8 weeks before last frost. Transplant after last frost in your area. Plant prefers full sun but will tolerate partial shade. Grows best in moderately moist soil. Put an inch of compost around base of plant each spring. Space plants 1 foot apart. Usually pest and disease free. Harvest leaves for drying before plant blooms, otherwise harvest anytime. Gather them in the morning. Cut flowers for drying when they are ¾ open. Take leaves by starting at the bottom of the plant. Hang upside down to dry, the flowers that is. This plant is a bees favorite.

BASIL: is an annual plant. There are many types of Basil. They grow anywhere from 1 to 2 feet tall. That have spikes of small white, pink or purple flowers that bloom mid-summer to fall. Sweet Basil has deep green, glossy leaves with smooth edges. Purple Ruffles Basil has purple frilled leaves with toothed edges. Anise Basil has green leaves with purple veins. Lemon Basil has small, sharply pointed, light green leaves with smooth edges. East Indian Basil leaves are covered with tiny gray hairs that make them look like soft felt. There are several more types of Basil all of them useful culinary herbs. Use fresh, dried or frozen with shellfish, egg dishes, soups, pasta, salads, salad dressings, and anything containing tomatoes. Make into pesto. Can be added to vinegars. Combine with virgin olive oil to make a flavored cooking oil. Basil teas help digestion. Sprigs of Basil in an arrangement add a pleasant fragrance. For early harvesting plant seeds indoors 6 weeks before last frost. Transplant into garden after danger of frost is over. Basil requires well drained, moist, rich soil.. Mulch with straw to retain high moisture level. Space plants 12 to 18 inches apart. Basil has problems with aphids, slugs and leaf spot disease. Begin harvesting when plants are 8" tall and before they bloom. Harvest when leaves are dry. To make bushy cut back the central stem taking the top 2 or 3 sets of leaves. Cut off flower spikes as soon as they appear. Hang to air dry, but tastes better when frozen. Blanch leaves before freezing in ice cubes. Basil repels many flying insects, so use in arrangements, crush leaves to release there fragrance.

BAY: is a perennial plant it grows in zone 8. It can grow to 10 feet tall. In a pot 5 feet. Leaves are shiny, dark green, leathery with wavy edges, 1½ to 3½ inches long, ½ -1½ inches wide, short stalks. It has small inconspicuous greenish, yellow flower in small umbels from the leaf axil. Dark purple or black, one seeded, berries. Blooms in spring. Bay has many uses. A tea of the leaves can soothe the stomach and relieve gas. It is used in many dishes in the kitchen. It helps soothe the skin in bath water. Bay leaf helps repel insects in flour, put a leaf in with your flour. Bay needs a moderately rich well drained soil. Full sun to partial shade. Cuttings from fresh green shoots seem to be the best way to start a Bay, however it may take 6 to 9 months to root. Bay leaves may be harvested and dried throughout the year. Pick them early in the day To prevent curling put an object on top, maybe a board.

BEE BALM: is a perennial and grows in zones 3-9. Bee Balm will grow 3 to 5 feet tall. Tubular flowers bloom in showy tiered whorls at stem tips for several weeks in mid-summer. Colors range from white to pink, purple and red. Leaves are dark green with toothed edges. Bee Balm smells and tastes like mint with a citrus undertone. In cooking, sprinkle flowers in salads, dried leaves are good in teas. Bee Balm is said to help the growth of tomatoes and peppers. Start Bee Balm seeds indoors 8 weeks before last spring frost. Bee Balm prefers partial shade but will tolerate full sun. Plant in well drained, moist, fertile soil. Apply ½ inch of compost each spring. Bee Balm spreads rapidly so mulch surrounding area to control spreading. Usually pest free but can get powdery mildew. Harvest small amounts of leaves when dry. For drying in quantity, cut leaves before bloom in early summer, and again in late august early September. Cut flowers for drying when fully open.

BETONY: is a perennial and grows in zones 4-8. Betony grows 2-3 feet tall. Spikes of pinkish purple flowers bloom in mid-summer. Leaves are bright green with notched edges. Dies back in winter. Betony tastes and smells like black tea. Betony tastes like black tea but has no caffeine. It is said to relieve tension headaches, can also ease throat irritations and diarrhea. Sow Betony seeds indoors 6 weeks before last frost. Plant outdoors after last frost. Betony prefers partial shade but will tolerate full sun. Moderatley moist soil average fertility. Mulch with ½ inch compost every other year. Space plants 12 inches apart. Betony is generally pest free. Susceptible to root rot in soggy soil. For best quality gather leaves in morning when dew is dry. Gather in July before blooms, for best quality. Cut stems several inches above soil line and snip leaves off. Hang upside down to air dry.

BORAGE: is an annual but self seeds. Borage grows 3 feet tall. Flowers are clear blue star shaped, about ¼ inch in diameter, bloom in dropping clusters from mid-summer to frost. Leaves are broad and hairy and have prominent veins. Borage leaves and flowers have a salty close to cucumber taste. Mince leaves and add to yogurt, soups, salads and in chicken and fish dishes. A tea is said to be slightly laxative. Sow Borage indoors 6 to 8 weeks before last frost. Borage prefers full sun but tolerates partial shade. Plants generally do best in cool temperatures. Plant in moist, fertile well drained soil. Allow 2 feet for each plant. Usually pest free. Will get root rot in soggy soil. Harvest leaves anytime, in growing season, when dew is dry. Pick flowers when fully open and dry. Snip individual leaves or strip off cut stems. Freeze Borage flowers in ice cubes for a decorative touch to iced drinks. Bees love Borage.

CARAWAY: is annual or biannual and grows in zones 3-9. Annuals grow to 2 feet, biannual to 8 inches the first year, to 2 feet the second year. Flowers are flat Queen Anne's lace like umbrels of tiny white flowers blooming in late summer. Biennials bloom in their second year. The ferny green leaves resemble those of carrots. Biennials die back in winter but sprout again in the second spring. Caraway seeds and roots have a sharp spicy taste and fragrance while the leaves taste like dill. In cooking use the fresh leaves in soups, stews and salads. Add seeds to breads and salad dressings. A mild tea can be made by steeping, soaking, crushed caraway seeds in water or milk to help digestion. Sow seeds in the garden as soon as soil can be worked in spring. Caraway prefers full sun but will tolerate partial shade. Prefers sandy, well drained, slightly dry soil, however the plant will suffer if the surface of the soil dries out below the first inch, so scratch ½ inch of compost into first couple of inches of soil before planting.

Space plants 6 to 8 inches apart. Caraway is inclined to have aphids and carrot weevils. Can develop crown rot. Harvest leaves anytime after plant is 5 to 6 inches tall. Harvest seeds when they are ripe. Gather both only when completely dry. Harvest roots in fall. Cut leaves at their base or strip off cut stems. When seed heads begin opening enclose them in a paper sack and cut off entire seed head.

CATNIP: is a perennial and grows in zones 3-9. It grows from 2 to 3 feet tall. Flowers are spikes of pinkish, purple or white, they bloom in mid-summer. Leaves are opposite with toothed margins and heart shaped leaves about 2 to 3 inches long. Both stems and leaves are covered with downy soft hairs. Plants die back over the winter. In teas Catnip is more mellow than Peppermint. Catnip can be added to salads. Start with a few fresh leaves to see if you like it. Otherwise good in teas. Fresh or dried leaves, the tea is good for digestion and may help in getting a good nights sleep. Sow seeds in garden a couple of weeks before last spring frost. Plant in full sun. Catnip prefers moist well drained soil. Scratch about a ½ inch of compost into the top few inches of soil before planting seeds. Space the plants 8 to 10 inches apart. Only pest problem is that the cats may nibble the leaves. The plant may get root rot. When harvesting to dry, cut whole stems with flower stalks, about 2 inches from soil surface. Hang upside down to air dry or strip leaves and flowers from stems and dry in dehydrator. If harvesting for medicinal uses or for your cat wait until plant blooms. Always gather in the morning after the dew has dried. Here's a little tip. To keep your Catnip safe from cats enclose plant in chicken wire cage till it is well established.

CHAMOMILE: There are 2 kinds of Chamomile, German Chamomile and Roman Chamomile. German grows 2 to 3 feet tall and is an annual. Roman grows 8 to 10 inches tall and is a perennial. They grow in zones 5 to 9. Both Chamomiles make excellent teas that are said to help one sleep. Chamomile has an erect, much branched, cylindrical stem and light green leaves that are finely divided and almost feathery-looking. Single daisy like flower heads that grow on long stalks and have yellow centers and white petals. The blooms have an apple like smell. Sow both types of Chamomile when soil is about 55 to 60 degrees, fahrenheit that is. Both plants prefer full sun but will tolerate partial shade. Well drained sandy soils. Scratch in ½ inch of compost in the top few inches of soil before planting. Allow 6 to 8 inches between plants. Harvest when flowers are fully open, will be late spring and early summer for German and slightly earlier for Roman. Clip off flowers and dry on a screen or in dehydrator.

CHERVIL: Annual, 12 to 18 inches tall. Tiny white flowers in Queen Anne's lace like umbrels in early summer. Green ferny like leaves resemble those of carrots. Tastes like mild licorice and young parsley. Chervil is good in soups, stews, salads and potato dishes, and any foods you would use parsley in. Add leaves to cooked foods just before serving so as not to loose flavor. Chervil requires rich moist soil. Apply ½ inch compost before seeding. Space plants 6 to 8 inches apart. In the north plant in full sun. In southern areas and for second planting in the north, choose a location with filtered shade. Chervil is intolerant to heat. Begin harvesting leaves when plants are 6 inches tall. Gather leaves in morning before the plant blooms. Cut outside stems at node [where leaf branch attaches to stem]. Pinch out flower stalks to prolong harvest.

CHIVES: Perennial, 12 to 18 inches tall. Grows in zones 3 to 10. Chives have globe shaped clusters of pink to purple flowers in mid spring. Garlic chives bear loose clusters of star shaped white or mauve flowers in late summer. Chives have hollow cylindrical leaves. Garlic chives have flat leaves. Both die back in fall. Snip leaves into salads, soups and egg dishes. Sprinkle over cooked fish and other entrees to add flavor and appearance. Toss whole flowers into salads. Plant Chives in full sun to partial shade. Sow in early spring. Divide chives every 3 years to prevent overcrowding. In early spring or early fall, dig the clump with a spade. Trim the roots to about 3 inches long and the tops to about 2 inches. Gently pull the clump into sections of 4 to 6 bulbs each. Replant 8 to 12 inches apart. Harvest after leaves are at least 6 inches tall. Cut leaves with a sharp knife or shears at least 2 inches above the soil. Snip off flowers just after they are fully open. Cut back chives after flowering.

CILANTROL/ CORIANDOR; is an annual that grows 2 to 3 feet tall. Cilantrol has flat white to pinkish umbrels that resemble parsley. Flowers bloom about 3 to 4 months after sowing. Its ferny leaves resemble those of flat leaved parsley. Cilantrol is vital in salsa and many tomato sauces, particularly those made for Mexican, Asian or east Indian dishes, with cooked beans, rice, fish and poultry. Use fresh leaves in salads. Use seeds in curries and with fish, poultry and legumes. Cilantro does not transplant well. Start in peat or newspaper pots about 6 weeks before last spring frost or sow directly in garden after last frost. Plant in full sun. Prefers well drained moist soil. Space plants 8 to 10 inches apart. Harvest when plant is 5 to 6 inches tall. Gather leaves in the morning in spring and summer before plant blooms. Harvest seeds [called Coriander], when dry and fully ripe, summer through fall. Cut off leaf stems where leaf attaches to stem, taking outside leaves first Enclose ripening seed heads to prevent them from dropping. Remove entire seed head.

CLARY: Biennial grows 2½ to 3 feet tall in zones 4 to 7. Clary has pink to purple-blue or white bracts surround the small flowers which grow in spikes blooming in mid to late summer. Gray- green leaves are downy with slightly toothed edges. Tastes like culinary sage, but leaves can be bitter if used in to great a quantity. In cooking use as you would sage, season breads, stuffing, cheese and veggie dishes. Freeze seeds for 3 to 5 days before planting. Can start indoors 8 weeks before last spring frost or direct plant in garden once soil has warmed. Plant in full sun. Clary grows best in well drained soil. Let top inch or 2, of soil, dry between waterings. Space plants 9 to 12 inches apart. Pick leaves when dew is dry anytime during growing season. Cut flowering stems when flowers are ¾ open. Snip leaves, or cut whole stems of flowers, near the base of plant. After first winter frost cut stems of first year plants to 1 inch above soil. Mulch heavily to protect roots over winter.

DILL: is an annual it grows 1½ to 5 feet tall and is self sewing. The flowers are flat umbrels about 6 inches across with many tiny yellowish flowers. Dill has ferny thread like blue-green foliage. Dill has many culinary uses. Use leaves or seeds to flavor cheeses, fish, poultry,beef, egg, bean, pea or veggie dishes. Complimentary to almost all cabbage family veggies. Tasty in green salads with cukes and sliced tomatoes. Sow directly in garden after last spring frost. Plant in full sun. Dill grows best in moist well drained soil. Allow 6 to 8 inches between plants. Cut leaves after plants are 6 inches tall gathering them in morning after dew dries, summer to early fall. Cut leaves for drying just before plant blooms. Collect seed heads for pickles from the time flowers are fully open. Harvest ripe seeds for drying. Snip off individual leaves when plant is young. Cut whole stems of foliage for drying and strip leaves off. For use in pickles cut off seed heads with an inch of stem attached.

FENNEL: is a perennial that grows 2 to 5 feet tall in zones 6 to 9. Flowers are 6 inch wide umbrels of tiny yellow flowers that appear mid-summer. The leaves are feathery blue-green that look a lot like dill. Fennel leaves and seeds have a mild licorice or anise flavor. Snip fresh leaves or mince stems and add to salads, or over fish, pork, eggs, cheese, beans, rice and cabbage family veggies. Add seeds to Asian dishes, sauerkraut, fish, lentils, breads, butter and cheese. Fennel flavor fades quickly when heated so add to recipe just before serving. Sow Fennel directly in garden a week or 2 before last spring frost. South of zone 5 you can also plant fennel in fall. Fennel prefers full sun but will tolerate partial shade. Fennel requires moderately fertile well drained soil. Will not tolerate over watering. Space plants 6 inches apart. Harvest leaves before the plant blooms gathering in the morning when dew is dry. Collect ripe seeds on a dry day. Cut whole stems of leaves for drying. Enclose ripening seed heads in paper bags to prevent seeds from scattering. Remove whole seed heads.

LEMON BALM: is a perennial that grows 1 to 2 feet tall in zones 4 to 9. Lemon Balm has clusters of ½ inch long tubular whitish flowers, bloom in mid-summer, where the leaves join the stems. The opposite leaves are a bright green and have toothed edges. Plants die back over winter. Use minced fresh lemon balm in salads, sauces, sauerkraut and stuffing and sprinkle over veggies, chicken and fish dishes. Makes a good tea. Sow seeds in garden about 2 weeks before last spring frost. Divide plants in spring or early summer, replant and water well. Plant in well drained soil. Plants spaced 11/2 to 2 feet apart. Snip off stem tips when harvesting small amounts of leaves. For drying quantity, cut whole stems 4 inches above soil line.

LEMON GRASS: Perennial that grows 3 to 5 feet tall and spreads up to 4 feet wide. Grows in zones 9 to 10. Lemon grass rarely flowers, when it does it has inconspicuous greenish flowers that form at the top of the stalk. Strap like leaves grow in a grassy clump. The base of each leaf is enlarged and whitish colored. North of zone 9 winter indoors. Use leaves fresh, dried or frozen and the bulbous stems, in Thai- Vietnamese dishes, stir fries, soups, pasta, tofu and veggies. Start seeds in pots or seedling flats in early spring. Transplant after danger of frost is over. Divide roots into 2 or 3 pieces. Plant in spring or early summer Lemon grass prefers full sun in rich moist soil. Space plants 2 to 4 feet apart. Harvest leaves and stems anytime once the plants are 1 feet tall. Gently pull off older outside bulbous stems from base for use in cooking.

The young leaves can also be cut off and used. Snip off leaves for tea making.

LEMON VERBENA: Perennial grows 2 feet tall and wide in zones 9 and 10.Flowers in late summer to early fall, tall spikes of tiny, tubular, lavender-colored flowers, grow where the leaves join the stem. Narrow pointed leaves grow in whorls of 3 or 4. Some plants have slightly hairy leaves. Stems become woody with age. Add the lemon flavored leaves to sauces, marinades and salad dressings. Use fresh leaves in fruit salads, deserts and beverages. Seeds are hard to find and difficult to germinate, so best to buy a plant. Lemon Verbena prefers full sun. Plant in fertile soil. Space plants 12 inches apart. Harvest leaves and stems anytime after plant reaches 8 inches tall. Cut whole stems for drying large quantities.

LOVAGE: is a perennial that grows 6 feet tall and 2 to 3 feet wide in zones 4 to 8.Umbrels of tiny yellowish white flowers appear in mid to late summer. Glossy compound, celery like leaves grow from thick stalks. Plants die back in winter. Lovages flavor and fragrance strongly resemble celery. Use celery flavored leaves, fresh, frozen or dried, anywhere you would use celery, particularly in cheese and egg dishes and soups and stews. Include fresh leaves in salads.Plant seeds immediately, or buy plants. Plant in garden just before last frost or in late summer. Lovage prefers partial or filtered shade, will tolerate full shade. Plant in well drained moist soil Allow 2 square feet per plant. Harvest leaves anytime for immediate use. For best quality gather after morning dew is dry. Harvest leaves for drying before plant flowers. Harvest entire ripe seed heads In late summer. Snip off leaves as needed.

If harvesting for drying, cut 1 to 3 foot sections of the stem. Lovage loses flavor unless it is dried quickly, so use a dehydrator.

MARJORAM, sweet: Is a perennial that grows to 1 foot tall in zones 9 and 10. Clustered flower spikes appear in late summer to early fall. The flower buds look like knots before they open into tiny white or pink blooms. The leaves are opposite fuzzy, oval leaves, from ¼ to 1 inch long. Use fresh leaves in salads or for garnishes. Marjoram is somewhat milder and sweeter than oregano. Use fresh, frozen or dried wherever you would use oregano. Good for seasoning cheese, beef, pork, cabbage and family veggies. Start seeds indoors. Sweet Marjoram is slow to germinate and tiny when young. Transplant in garden after all chances of frost is past. Sweet Marjoram prefers full sun but tolerates partial shade. Plant in sandy well drained soil. Allow top inch of soil to dry between waterings. Space plants 6 to 8 inches apart. Pick individual leaves after plant is 6 to 8 inches tall. Best done after morning dew is dry. Cut stems with leaves before plant blooms for drying. Snip branch tips when taking for immediate use.

MINTS: are perennials Grow up to 2 feet tall, depending on the species. They grow in zones 5 to 9. Mints have spikes of purple, pink or white flowers that bloom above the leaves in mid to late summer. They have opposite leaves in many shades of green, most with toothed edges, cover characteristic square stems. Plants die back over winter. Mints compliment the flavor of meat, fish and veggies. Use fresh leaves in salads, and add fresh or dried leaves to lamb stews, dried beans or cooked grains. Mint heightens the flavor of peas, new potatoes and carrots. Mints make a delicious tea. Purchase plants. Plant in garden anytime from early spring through late summer. Take cuttings from established plants before they bloom. Mints prefer partial or filtered shade but tolerate full sun or shade. Mints grow best in moist soil. Start plants 18 to 24 inches apart. Mints spread very fast and will take over the garden. Gather leaves from mint anytime after plant is 6 to 8 inches tall. Gather leafy stems after dew dries. For drying , pick before or after plant blooms. Snip off the tips of branches. For drying, cut stems 4 to 6 inches above the soil surface during early summer, and make second cutting 1 inch above soil surface in fall.

OREGANO: is a perennial that grows 2 feet tall in zones 5 to 9. Culinary Oregano bears spikes of tiny white flowers above the leaves in mid-summer. Oregano leaves are carried on square stems they are opposite with toothed or smooth edges, and range from ½ to 2 inches long. Use the leaves, fresh or dried, to season cheeses, eggs, most veggies and meats. Oregano tea clears the nasal passages and eases the sore throat of the common cold. Grow seeds indoors 6 to 8 weeks before last spring frost. Transplant in garden a week before last frost. Propagate by layering. Bend stems to the ground and cover them with soil in early summer, transplant the newly rooted plants in early fall. Take cuttings in late spring, before bloom. Cut small sprigs anytime after the plant reaches 6 inches tall. Harvest whole stems for drying just before bloom. Cut the entire plant back to 2 to 3 inches above ground in August to promote new growth. Oregano prefers full sun. Plant in well drained soil, allow top inch of soil to dry out between waterings. Plant 1 foot apart.

Snip off the ends of stems with sharp scissors. For drying cut off whole stems an inch or two above soil surface.

PARSLEY: is a Biennial that grows 8 to 12 inches tall in zones 5 to 9. Queen Anne's lace like umbrels of tiny greenish yellow flowers bloom in late spring in the second year of growth. Curly parsley has fine, ferny, curled and ruffled, deep green leaves that are held on long stems from the top of the plant. The foliage of flat leaf parsley resembles celery. Add fresh, frozen or dried leaves to soups, stews casseroles, veggie dishes, fish and poultry. Use fresh leaves in salads or as a garnish. Chewing a sprig after you eat cleans and freshens your breath. So eat your little green trees after your meal and you'll smell sweet as can be. Parsley is best started from plants, seeds are very hard to start. Parsley prefers full sun but will tolerate partial to full shade. Needs well drained moist soil. Space plants 10 to 12 inches apart. Harvest leaves anytime after plant has 8 leaves. Cut off stems and leaves 1 inch above crown of plant. Dry parsley in a dehydrator for best flavor and color.

ROSEMARY: is a perennial that grows 2 to 6 feet tall in zones 8 to 10. Tiny pink to purple flowers bloom in clusters of 2 to 3 along the branches in late winter to early spring. Rosemary's leaves are needle like and leathery ½ to 1½ inch long. Use fresh or dried with pork, lamb, poultry, fish, tofu, eggs, cheese, breads, stuffing's and veggies. Rosemary prefers full sun but will tolerate partial shade. Needs extremely well drained soil. Allow top of soil, about 1 inch, to dry before watering. Allow 1 to 3 feet between plants. Harvest stems and leaves anytime for small amounts. For large amounts, cut stems back to within 1 or 2 leaf nodes above woody growth. Dry on flat screens or in dehydrator.

SAGE: is a perennial that grows 2½ to 3 feet tall in zones 4 to 8. Small pink, purple, blue or white tubular flowers grow in whorls of 4 to 8 at points where leaves attach to stems. They bloom in late spring to early summer. Leaves are gray-green 2 inches long and maybe hairy, velvety, or pebbly looking. Use fresh or dried leaves in stuffing, breads, veggies, tofu, cheese and many meats. Freeze seeds for 3 days before planting. Plant seeds in garden 2 weeks before last spring frost. Sage prefers full sun. Plant in well drained soil 2 feet apart. Pick individual leaves anytime. Harvest quantities of leaves for drying in mid to late summer. Cut whole branches back to within one to two pairs of leaves above where the stems become woody. Hang upside down to air dry.

SAVORY, summer: is an annual that grows 18 inches tall. Its white or pale pink, ¼ inch flowers bloom in groups of 3 to 6 at upper leaf axils [where the leaves join the stems] from mid summer until frost. The leaves are narrow 1 inch long and gray-green in color. Use fresh or dried leaves to season beans of all kinds. Savory is also good with cheeses, eggs, cabbage family crops, parsnips, squash, chicken, fish and soups. Sow seeds in garden 1 week before last spring frost. Prefers full sun, well drained soil, keep moderately moist. Space plants 10 inches apart. Pick small sprigs after plant is 6 to 8 inches tall. Harvest stems for drying before plant flowers. Harvest in morning after dew has dried. Cut off stem tips for small amounts. For drying cut off whole stems several inches above soil surface. Hang stems upside down to air dry, or dry on screens.

SAVORY, winter: is a perennial that grows 16 inches tall in zones 5 to 10.Spikes of small white to purplish flowers bloom atop plants in early summer. Leaves are a 1 inch narrow oval with smooth edges wider at the tip than at the base. Winter Savory is semi-evergreen in moderate climates. This strong flavored herb is best used in crab dishes and with other strong flavors. It overpowers chicken but is just right in pates and meat pies. Buy young plants and plant in spring or summer. Prefers full sun but will tolerate filtered shade. Prefers well drained light soil. Space plants 1 foot apart. Harvest small sprigs as needed. For drying before or after the plant blooms. For best quality, gather leafy stems after morning dew dries. Cut whole stems 6 inches above soil surface, cut again near end of summer. Hang stems upside down to air dry.

SWEET CICELY: is a perennial that grows 3 feet tall in zones 3 to 7. Queen Anne's like lace umbrels of tiny white flowers bloom in May or June. The leaves are ferny, finely lobed or toothed leaflets of clear green with whitish undersides. The leaf stalks wrap around the stem of the plant. Use fresh leaves in salads and with fruits. The dried or frozen leaves are excellent with fish. Use seeds in cakes or deserts. Cook fresh or dried roots like a parsnip or add to soups and stews. Buy young plants and plant in spring or summer. Sweet Cicely prefers shade or partial shade, will die in full sun. Plant in rich, moist, well drained soil. Add ½ inch of compost every spring. Space plants 2 inches apart. Pick Sweet Cicely leaves anytime. Harvest seeds on a midsummer afternoon when they are ripe and dry. Dig roots after they are 1 year old. For drying cut whole stems. Enclose seed heads before seeds begin to brown and cut them with a length of stem just as they begin to shatter. Hang stems upside down to dry leaves or bagged seed heads..

TARRAGON, FRENCH; is a perennial that grows 2 feet tall in zones 4 to 8. Tiny round inconspicuous flowers bloom on stem tips in midsummer. Narrow smooth edged leaves are 1 to 4 inches long. They grow in groups of 3 at the base of the plant and singly at the top. Use fresh Tarragon in salads [sparingly, it's strong] and in sauces. Use in meat or poultry dishes. Add Tarragon at very end of cooking time to avoid bringing out a bitter taste. Buy a young plant and plant in spring or summer. Divide plants in early spring after they are 3 years old. Prefers full sun, tolerates filtered shade. Needs well drained fertile soil. Apply ½ inch of compost in early spring each year. Allow 2 square feet for each plant. Pick leaves anytime, for best flavor in the morning. For drying cut whole branches. Use a dehydrator as Tarragon loses quality unless dried rapidly.

THYME; is a perennial that grows 6 to 15 inches tall in zones 5 to 9. Clusters of tiny pink to purple tubular blooms at the stem tips in midsummer. Most Thymes have small, ¼ to ½ inch, narrow leaves, with a pale hairy underside and smooth edges. Thyme goes with almost everything. Fresh leaves are a nice addition to a salad. Try fresh or dried with seafood, poultry, veggies, legumes, cheeses, eggs, rice and tomato sauce. Frozen sprigs are handy for soups and stews. Plant plants in early spring. Divide plants in spring or fall. Thyme prefers full sun but will tolerate partial shade. Plant in well drained light soil. Harvest leaves in morning when plants are not in bloom. Snip off stem tips. For drying cut entire plant back to 2 inches above soil just before it blooms. Enclose bunched stems and hang upside down in paper sacks to air dry, or place stems on fruit leather insert in dehydrator.

CHAPTER 10

Edible Flowers And Plants

Edible Flowers And Plants.

I was told that as a child I loved to go into the garden, and always came back with a yellow nose. This happened so much my aunt said she was afraid it would turn yellow forever. She was chuckling when she said this. It seems I loved to smell the flowers and plants, and did so by sticking my nose into them as far as I could. That way I could get the very best smell. I still love to smell the flowers and plants but have learned that bees and wasps have priority. They do the work of pollinating and making honey. They leave enough scent for me. Flowers and plants are not just pretty they have vitamins that are good for us, and some are quite tasty too. Roses, the rosehip, fruit of the plant, is rich in vitamin C, also vitamins A, B, E, and K, organic acids and pectin. The acids and pectin make rosehips mildly laxative and diuretic. Violets have an abundance of vitamins A and C. They can help food be more pleasing to the eye and still smell pretty. So no I don't have a yellow nose, and have learned to give bees, wasps and humming birds priority. I still love to see and smell the beauty of the earth, and am now learning how to use it for our benefit.

CAYENNE PEPPER; is a perennial that grows to 1 foot tall. This is an unusual looking plant. It has angular hardwood branches and stems that have a slightly purplish cast. The flowers are in pairs, or clusters on long stems. The greenish or yellowish white flowers often have reddish or golden vein like markings across 5 bluish stamens. The leaves are broad, puffy and wrinkled looking can be either hairless or downy 3 to 6 inches long. The fruit is pod like. Shiny leathery covering of varying shades of red, orange and yellow when ripe. Grows to 2 feet or more. Medicinally herbalists have used Cayenne for relief from gas, diarrhea and toothaches. Add a pinch of cayenne to native American, Cajun, Creole, Spanish, Mexican, S.E. Asian, and east Indian recipes, or to egg dishes, cheeses, creamy soups and sauces, curries and chili blends. Omit cayenne from recipes that will be frozen as it gets to intense instead add when ready to serve. Cayenne is native to the tropics it can be grown in temperate climates where you can grow tomatoes and eggplants. It likes full sun and a fertile moist soil. Best to start indoors from seed. Plant outdoors 2 weeks after last frost. Set young plants 12 to 18 inches apart. Needs plenty of water. Straw mulch will help protect during hot summers. Peppers are ready to harvest when fruit has turned bright red. Don't pull off, cut stems ½ inch from pepper cap. Hot peppers keeps best if dried immediately. Can dry by hanging upside down or in a dehydrating.

CHICORY; is a perennial and grows 3 to 5 tall is hardiest in zone 3. Flowers are dandelion like sky blue, 1 to 1 ½ inches wide, has ray flowers that close at midday. The leaves are broad oblongs with ragged indentations, hairy, large at bottom of plant, diminishing in size to the top of the plant. The fruits are hard and brownish red in color, about a tenth of an inch long. Chicory supposedly smoothes out coffee. Added to coffee it has much less effect on the nervous system and heart. The leaves are similar to dandelions and can be used cooked or fresh like spinach. The root is used dried in hot beverages. Chicory root is a mild tonic, diuretic and laxative. Chicory will grow in average to poor well drained soil. Prefers full sun.

Grows well in same place that carrots do.. Direct seed in early spring. Thin seedlings to about 1 foot apart. Pamper by pulling weeds as soon as they appear. Water attentively if weather turns dry. By fall you should have a root to dig, or leave to develop next year. Fall is the time to think of forcing the roots for winter greens. Young leaves can be harvested for salads in spring. The root is dug in fall and dried roasted and ground for use in beverages.

CINNAMON; is a perennial and grows in tropical climate this is a fast growing tree that will grow 7 to 10 feet tall. Cinnamon is a small tender evergreen that can be grown in the south. Flowers are inconspicuous yellowish long panicles. Leaves are bright red turning green with maturity, glossy ovate lancelet 7 inches long. Research has shown that cinnamon kills fungi, bacteria and other microorganisms including one that causes botulism. The part of the plant that is used is the inner bark. As it dries it curls into sticks. Sticks can be used whole or ground. It can be used with meats or in deserts. It's versatility extends from fruit pies to meat pies. Add ground cinnamon to tomato sauce, it brings out their sweetness. Plant in the south in well drained, sandy loam with plenty of nutrients because they are fast growing trees. Propagation is by seeds or cuttings. Start in spring in a hot bed. The inner bark is used for the spice. As it dries it curls into sticks. Generally grown as bushes, 10 feet tall, as the stems are continually cut back to produce new stems for bark. The outer bark, cork and the pithy inner lining are scraped off and the remaining bark is left to dry completely.

CLOVES; is a perennial non-hardy woody tree that grows in zone 10. It needs humidity and grows 15 to 20 feet tall. Clove is a non-hardy, woody, evergreen tree. The trunk divides into larger branches covered in smooth gray bark. Flowers grow in clusters of white through peach pink to red tinged. Petal tips form a hood shrouding many stamens. Leaves are oblong lance shaped 5 inches long, glossy green, veined and sometimes hairy. The fruit is a long berry. The clove is a temporary help for a toothache. A whole clove held on the tooth helps numb it. The small dried buds, whole or ground, are used in cooking. Whole ones are generally removed before serving. Cloves are great with beets, green beans, carrots, squash, split pea soup, mixed winter fruit salads, fruit compotes, rhubarb, prunes, cranberries, pickling brines, strong meat stews, cakes, puddings, mincemeats, marinades, spiced teas and mulled beverages. Cloves must have a warm, wet, steamy climate. Ordinary soil. Plant needs full sun. The unopened flower bud is the part used when dried.

COFFEE; is a perennial tree that grows 15 to 40 feet tall in zone 10. During fruit bearing season coffee is a pretty sight. Coffee fruit ripens in succession over a long period. Sometimes the branches are clotted with green and red berries and bunches of little white flowers. Coffees are evergreens and may live 100 years. Flowers grow in small clusters of delicate star shaped white flowers. Leaves are bright green on upper side and pale on underside. About 2½ inches wide and 6 inches long evergreen. The fruit is referred to as a berry, round, smooth, glossy, deep red when ripe. Coffee is a stimulating drink hot or cold. Coffee sprouts readily from seeds. It requires warmth and humidity. The temps must not drop below 60 degrees.

A How-to Book for Hard Times

Atmosphere must be humid, plant needs as much light as possible. Coffee plants like fertile soil, moist, rich, and well drained with high organic content. If conditions become to dry the plant will get scrawny, leaves will yellow and fall off. Plants should be given liquid fertilizer regularly. Coffee plants don't do well in houses as the air is to dry. Harvest the berries when they are deep red. Peel skin off two flat seeds with a grove running lengthwise down one side, enclosed in silvery parchment like skin. Remove this skin before roasting.

COMFREY; This plant is for EXTERNAL USE ONLY. It is a perennial that grows 3 to 5 feet tall in zones 7 to 9. Flowers are blue, yellow or whitish tubular about ½ inch long with 5 stamens. Leaves are deep green hairy and lance shaped up to 10 inches long. External use only, for bruises and external wounds and sores this herb is an effective remedy. Fresh leaves can be mashed with a blender and applied to the skin. Do not boil comfrey, high temperature breaks down its medicinal value. You can start Comfrey by seed or cutting anytime. Set plants 3 feet apart. Choose location carefully as once it is established you're not getting rid of it. Requires no maintenance once established. Will do well in moist rich soil, in full sun to partial shade. Harvest the leaves in spring. Dry them and store in a tightly sealed container.

DANDELION; is not just a weed. It is a perennial that grows 6 inches to 1 foot tall, and it grows everywhere. I think everyone knows what a dandelion looks like, but just in case; Flowers are golden yellow, 1½ to 2 inches across, on a smooth, hollow stem. The petals close in the evening and open at daylight. Leaves are 2 to 2½ inches long, very jagged, fleshy, smooth mostly hairless and dark green. Grows in rosettes close to the ground. Flowers in late spring, Turns into a fluffy, down like puffball that carry the seeds on the wind in fall. Dandelion wine is supposedly good for the blood. Many parts of the world roast the root and use as an addition to coffee and cocoa. Young tender leaves are used in salads. Older leaves are steamed or sautéed like spinach. Flowers can be used as a garnish or to lend color to herb vinegar. Dandelions will grow anywhere and require no attention. Harvesting depends on the part of the plant you're going to use. Fresh flowers are used to make dandelion wine. Leaves taken in spring need to be blanched to reduce their bitterness. If you don't want to use them right away store in the refrigerator as you would any salad green. The larger leaves, harvested in fall, are less bitter and don't need blanching.

ECHINACEA; is a perennial that grows 1 to 2 feet tall in zone 8. Flowers are purple cones that resemble a black eyed susan. Its sturdy stems are covered with tiny bristly hairs, its roots are long and black. Leaves are pale to dark green ovate, pointed, coarsely toothed, 3 to 8 inches long, upper leaves shorter and narrow. Blooms in mid to late summer. Echinacea is strictly medicinal. The root is the part of the plant used for its medicinal properties. It is considered to be the leading herb on the list of immune – stimulants. Echinacea needs a well drained soil. Prefers full sun but will tolerate light shade. Easy to start from seed but wait till temperatures are 70 degrees before you sow. Space 11/2 to 2 feet apart. Soil needs to be moderately moist. If you have cold dry winters cover the plant with hay or evergreens. Every 4 or 5 years dig up and replant in newly fertilized soil. If you intend to use the roots for herbal healing, it is best to wait until after the plant has had several hard frosts and begins to die back. The root should then be cleaned and dried. The crown of the plant can be replanted but wont be as medicinally potent.

ELECAMPANE; is a perennial it grows 4 to 6 feet tall in zone 8. Commonly known as a wild sunflower. Sturdy almost unbranching, the round stem is coarse and woody. Flowers resemble sunflowers 3 to 4 inches across. Leaves are toothed and bristly on upper surface, velvety on underside. They are oblong, pointed up to 2 feet long. The front is brown with a ring of pale reddish hairs. Elecampane is strictly medicinal. The root is used for treating ailments of the chest. Rarely used alone said to be an effective ingredient in many compound medicines. An American Indian remedy for treating bronchial and other lung ailments. Combine ½ lb. each of Elecampane root, Spikenard root, and Comfrey root. Mash the roots really well and combine with a gallon of water, boil down to a quart. Pour liquid off into a ½ gallon container, and add 8 ounces of alcohol and a pint and a half of honey. Recommend a teaspoon every 2 hours. Root stock is used in candy or as a sweet. Elecampane grows well in any garden soil, with a moist shady spot it will do well. Start from shoots or 2 inch root taken from mature plant in fall. Set out after frost has past. If you intend to harvest roots do so in the fall of the plants second year.

EUCALYPTUS; is a perennial tree that can grow up to 489 feet tall. They do grow in California, southern part. There are many kinds, more than 500 species ranging from a bushy 5 feet to towering 480 feet.giants. They have a strong fragrance. Most common the blue gum. The bark is a blue-gray in color. Flowers occur near leaf axils. The stamens maybe white, cream, pink, yellow, orange or red. Young leaves are opposite, broad, stalk less, silvery bluish gray; mature leaves alternate, stalked, sword like, thick, dark, lustrous green; 4 to 12 inches long. Fruit are capsules containing several seeds. Eucalyptus is strictly medicinal. You can use the oil as an antibacterial, do not use full strength, always dilute with water, vegetable oil, or rubbing alcohol, no more than 2 tsps of oil to a pint of liquid. Widely used for respiratory ailments. You can make a simple, usable, infusion at home by steeping a handful of fresh or dried leaves for 20 minutes in a quart of boiling water. Steeping means you put leaves into boiling water and remove from heat, right away. Cover and let stand for 20 minutes, for best results. Breathe in vapors of steaming tea. The tea can be drunk or used in a vaporizer. It is best to transplant a hardy young tree. Eucalyptus transplants easily. It prefers light loam but will adapt easily to most any soil. Eucalyptus is a heavy feeder and needs plenty of sun. To much water will make the leaves blister, so be careful not to over water. If Eucalyptus is grown outdoors it needs full sunlight and 50 degrees.

FLAX; grows up to 20 inches tall, grows in the North West and Canada. Flax grows in solitary erect stem that branches off at the top. Flowers are light blue, 5 petals, ½ inch across. They wither quickly after opening in morning. Leaves are alternate stalkless, pale green, spear shaped ¾ to 1 inch long. Fruit is a globular pod, contains 10 brown seeds about ¼ inch long. Flax has many uses. Grown for linseed oil, with fibers from the straw being used for fine papers. Medicinally use caution. Immature seed pods are poisonous. Overdose symptoms include gasping, weakness, paralysis and convulsion. So if not sure of maturity of seed DO NOT USE. A tea, made of mature seeds, is made with 1 ounce of ground or whole seeds to 1 pint of boiling water. Add a bit of honey and lemon for taste. Tea is a mild laxative. Culinary Flax has long been used as an ingredient in hearty breads. Flax likes a well drained soil with full sun to partial shade. It is easy to grow. Sow seeds in early spring or late fall and thin the seedlings to 4 inches apart. Be careful as flax has shallow roots. Do not fertilize till plant is fully grown, then use occasional dose of diluted liquid fertilizer. Seeds can be harvested at the same time as the fiber, just before the flower blooms. Either leave the Seeds to ripen on the cut sheaths, or allow them to mature fully on the plant, a while after the flower drops. The flax fibers are softer and stronger if harvested when blossoms have just fallen and stalk begins to turn yellow. Don't let seeds get damp as they will be damaged.

GARLIC; Grows to 2 feet tall anywhere you can grow onions. Garlic is made up of 4 to 15 cloves, or bulblets. Flowers are very small white to pinkish, six segments, six stamens in globe shaped umbrels. Leaves are 4 to 6 inches long and ½ inch wide. Garlic has many uses. It has been used to treat high blood pressure and other cardiac or circulatory ailments. It also helps in lowering cholesterol levels. Use as much as your friends can tolerate. Culinary Garlic is used in many ways. It adds dimension to all foods except deserts. Add minced garlic to herb butters, cheese spreads, breads, beans, broccoli, cauliflower, crackers, salads, stuffing, sauces, marinades, salad dressings, stews, soups, meats, fish, poultry, game, herb vinegars, flavored oils and pickles. Garlic will become bitter if burned. Roasting gives garlic a nutty flavor. Garlic cloves peel easily if you smash them first with the flat side of your knife. It is best to start garlic from cloves. Plant in early spring, in rich, deep, moist, well drained soil. It likes full sun to partial shade. Plant cloves 2 inches deep and about 6 inches apart. When flower stalks appear in early summer, cut them back so that the plant will use energy to develop bulbs. The tops should begin to bend and turn brown. If by midsummer they have not done this knock them down yourself. Withhold water for a few days and later lift the plants, wait just a couple of days before lifting plants. Place on a screen in the shade for several days, then shake dirt off. To store put in a cool, dry, dark place. Take care not to bruise bulbs. One easy attractive way to store garlic is to braid the leaves into a rope.

GINGER; is a tropical perennial plant that grows 2 to 4 feet tall. Flowers are dense cone like spikes 3 inches long at the end of a 6 to 12 inch stalk; corolla composed of 2¾ inch Male flowers yellow-green segments and one purple lip, spotted and striped with yellow; occur between 1 inch long, overlapping green bracts. Leaves are 6 to 12 inches long ¾ inch wide and grass like alternate, pointed, lance shaped. Rarely flowers in cultivation. Ginger is used for indigestion and to take the wind out of flatulence. In the winter a cup of ginger tea is warming and invigorating. Pour 1 pint of boiling water over 1 ounce of rhizome [root] and steep for 5 to 20 minutes. The root of the plant is used fresh or dried. Add it to beverages, fruit salads, meats, poultry, fish, preserves, pickles, sweet potatoes, winter squash, carrots, beets, pumpkin, rhubarb and peaches. Combine with onions and garlic. Ground ginger enhances sweet puddings, quick breads, muffins, cakes and cookies. Unless you have a tropical climate ginger grows easily in a container. Plant a rhizome in a large pot filled with equal parts loam, sand, peat moss and compost. Give it plenty of warmth, moisture and humidity. During warm months move the potted ginger to a semi shaded spot out doors. Leave in pot. To harvest, pull the plant from its pot 8 to 12 months after planting, cut off the leaf stalks and remove the fibrous roots. Cut off as much root as you can use and replant the rest.

GINSENG; is a perennial that grows 6 to 16 inches tall. Ginseng has a thin single stem that separates into compound leaves. The plants stem grows from a bud that forms on top of the root, after 3 or 4 years, 4 to 40 green flowers grow at center of umbrella; mostly in single umbrels ½ inch across. Young plants have one or two leaves, after 3 or 4 years, 3 to 6 leaves: each leaf divided into 5 toothed or lobed leaflets radiating from a central point. Fruit are bright red berries with 2 or 3 white seeds inside. The broadest health affect claimed for ginseng is that it is an adaptogen, a substance that protects against stress physical and mental. Put another way, adaptogens help body functions to return to normal more quickly than they would otherwise. Hence ginseng is supposed to increase physical endurance. Unless you have the naturally perfect garden spot, ginseng is very hard to grow. Ginseng needs humus rich, well drained loam in partial shade. Their native habitat is hardwood forests, making this a very difficult plant to grow.

HOP; is a perennial vine that grows 20 to 25 feet long and can grow to 40 feet in zone 8. This plant is a lot like a wild grape. The female plant flowers are inconspicuous, paired blooms on short spikes, grow into strobiles, which are cone like composed of overlapping, papery greenish white scales that contain the fruit. Male flowers are inconspicuous and white, they have 5 stamens and sepals in loose branches 3 to 5 inches long. Leaves resemble grape leaves, heart shaped, coarse, hairy, with finely serrated edges. Flowers in mid to late summer. The fruit is sprinkled with a yellow, grainy substance that is actually glandular hairs. Most common use for hops is in the making of beer. The vine can be used for basket weaving. Hops are started from cuttings or suckers from the healthiest older plants. Plant 6 feet apart in groups of 3 to 5 plants. Hops require deep, humus, well drained soil. You should dig deeply before planting. Train plants to long poles, wire or string. Major growth does not begin till second year and plant bears well in 3rd year and all the following years. Plants need full sun. Gather strobiles when they are amber brown and partly dry. Dry immediately after harvesting in an oven at 125 to 150 degrees. They lose their value if stored for a long time.

HOREHOUND; is a perennial that grows 2 to 3 feet tall. Horehound is part of the mint family and grows as a profusely as all mints. Flowers are white, tubular with 2 lips divided at margin into 10 hook like segments. Leaves opposite in pairs, lower ones stalked, 2 inches long, soft, hairy round to oval, serrated edges, upper surface veined, lower surface wooly. Fruit barbed seeds catch on clothing and animal fur. Clusters of 4, inside small nutlets at the base of spiny calyx. Horehound is valued as a cough soother. The furry leaves have a menthol-like taste, an infusion [tea] of them is the base for confections and throat lozenges. Candid horehound can be made by adding sugar to a strong tea of the leaves and boiling until the mixture reaches a thick consistency, strain into a shallow pan, cut into squares when cool. This makes your throat lozenges. Horehound grows easily, so easily it will take over if you don't restrict it. Maybe best confined to a pot. Start from seed sowing 1/8 inch deep in early spring. It takes a year for plant to reach maturity. Horehound does not produce flowers until the second year. The plant can be cut during the first year. Take only about a third of the plants top growth in the first year. You can hang branches to dry, but it loses its flavor quickly, to retain flavor remove leaves and chop them if using right away. To save put in tightly sealed jar.

HORSERADISH; grows 2 to 3 feet tall in its second year. Horseradish is part of the mustard family and is often grown as an annual to get the best quality root. Flowers are small white and grow at leaf axis. It has abundant leaves that are oblong and grow up to 1 foot long, upper ones are smaller, lance shaped and short stalked. Generally sterile but can produce good seeds after first year. Flowers in midsummer. Horseradish is a potent diuretic. A favorite way to take it when you want to flush fluids out of your system is to mix it with white wine. For culinary uses grating a fresh root and adding vinegar or mayonnaise is the usual way to use horseradish. Tender horseradish leaves can be added to a salad. To get plants you need a straight 8 to 9 inch long and ½ inch wide young root. Take time to prepare the soil ahead of planting. You will need a rich soil. Till deep and add compost. The root grows outward not downward so plant 12 to 18 inches apart. Horseradish spreads rapidly, will take over and is hard to get rid of. It likes a moist, rich, heavy soil and prefers full sun. You can begin harvesting horseradish root in late October or early November. You can pack the root in dry sand and keep in a cool dry place. Scrub the root before storing.

HYSSOP; is a perennial that grows 1½ to 3 feet tall in zones 4 to 9. Whorls of tiny purple or blue tubular flowers form on tall spikes in midsummer to early fall. Hyssops slender pointed leaves are smooth and opposite. Hyssop has a strong minty flavor, can become bitter if to much is used. Use flowers and leaves to give salads a cool minty flavor, also good in stuffing, other poultry dishes, soups, casseroles and fruit salads. For a nice tea add hyssop to one of the sweeter mints. Plant seed a week or two before last spring frost. Take cuttings in late spring or early fall and make root division in early spring or late summer. Hyssop prefers full sun but tolerates partial shade. Plant in well drained sandy soil. Let top inch of soil dry between waterings. Space plants 12 inches apart. Harvest leaves before the plant flowers, gather in morning when dew has dried. Pick flowers when blooms are ¾ open. Strip off portions of the stalk when harvesting a small amount for immediate use, strip the leaves from the stem. Cut whole branches for drying leaves or flowers. Good if you keep bees its nectar makes a fine honey.

LAVENDER; is a perennial that grows 3 feet tall in zones 5 to 8. Slender spikes of blue, purple, lavender, pink or white flowers in midsummer. Each flower spike maybe up to 1 foot tall. Lavenders opposite gray-green or silvery green leaves are narrow, smooth edged and somewhat hairy. Add fresh or dried flowers to baked goods and jellies. Mix the flowers with black tea for a fragrant cup. Start seeds indoors about 8 weeks before last spring frost. Transplant in garden after last spring frost. Lavender prefers full sun but will tolerate partial shade. Prefers well drained soil. Allow top inch to dry before watering again. Space plants 1 to 3 feet apart. Harvest flower spikes and stems when flowers are nearly open. Cut flowers several inches below the bloom. Hang to dry or use dehydrator.

LICORICE; is a perennial that grows 3 to 7 feet tall in California. Licorice is an erect, somewhat branching plant with a stringy root system. The flowers resemble sweet peas or vetch, ½ inch long purple or lavender spikes. Leaves are oblongs 1 to 2 inches long, yellow-green, lighter on underside and slightly damp and sticky. Licorice root is used to color and flavor a variety of things from tobaccos to just enjoying chewing the root itself. Medicinally it is used in cough drops and syrups. A stick cut from the root is satisfying to gnaw on and helps dieters and those trying to quit smoking. Licorice can be grown from seed but is usually started from dividing the root in early spring or late fall. Put cuttings 1 to 1½ feet apart in deeply tilled soil. It should be rich, mellow, moist and stone free. Water often after you set them out. Growth is slow for the first two years. Cut plants in late autumn or early winter when tops are dry. Dig a ditch to one side of plant and pull plant toward it. Shade dry root for 6 months. Moist roots are subject to mold. Should be stored in tightly closed containers.

MUSTARD; is an annual that grows 2 to 6 feet tall and grows anywhere. Mustard has four petaled flowers that form a maltese cross. Flowers are small, yellow crosses. Leaves are alternate, various shapes, lobed or coarsely toothed; upper leaves are less lobed. Fruit is a long slender pod. Mustard has both culinary and medicinal uses. Powdered seeds and oil can be irritating. Culinary use whole white or yellow seeds in making pickles or chutney. Black mustard seed to make mustard powder. Young leaves of black and white mustard are vitamin rich and tangy. An infusion [tea] of seeds added to a foot bath is supposed to sooth sore feet. A mustard plaster is an old cure for a congested chest. Do not leave the plaster on to long as it can blister. Should not be applied directly on the skin, instead put mustard plaster on a sheet of paper or cloth, then put the paper with plaster, or cloth on the chest. Remove as soon as it cools. Make sure no plaster remains. Mustard likes full sun and rich soil. Plant the tiny seeds 1/8 inch deep, sow in intervals from spring to early fall. Plant needs lots of nourishment so add well rotted manure, or finished compost, regularly to the soil. Mustard self sows so keep an eye that it doesn't take over the garden. Harvest seeds when pods have turned from green to brown. Cut and spread the pods on a screen or tray covered with a tightly woven cloth. In 2 weeks you'll find that the seeds ripen. Store whole or ground in tightly covered jars.

NASTURTIUM; is an annual plant that grows 1 foot tall but vines out to 6 feet. This is a flower and as with all flowers if you are going to use them for cooking or medicinal purposes use only ones that you have grown, that way you know they are free of any poisonous sprays or powders. Nasturtiums have cheery, open, funnel shaped flowers that bloom from summer through fall in colors from cream to brilliant reds, oranges and yellow. Each 5 petaled flower is 1½ to 2 inches across and has a long spur at the bottom. The leaves are round long stemmed with wavy or slightly lobed margins. Leaves can grow anywhere from 1 to 6 inches across depending on the soil. Nasturtium flowers and leaves taste spicy almost peppery with almost no fragrance. Use both leaves and flowers in fresh salads or as a garnish. Use preserved seed pods as a substitute for capers in tarter sauce and spiced mayo. Plant in garden after last spring frost. Nasturtiums prefer full sun. They will survive in filtered shade but don't flower as well. Plant in well drained soil. Space plants 12 inches apart. You can pick leaves as soon as plant is 6 inches tall. Pick flowers just as they open. Collect seed pods when they are ¼ inch in diameter. Cut leaves and flowers with their stems attached. Remove old flowers to extend bloom season. To collect seeds stop dead heading in mid august. Place fresh green seeds in a heat proof jar and pour heated vinegar over them. Let cure for a week before using. Store in fridge.

PENNYROYAL; is an annual plant of the mint family that grows 4 to 16 inches tall. There are 2 types of pennyroyal, American and European. Both belong to the mint family. The European is a perennial, American is an annual. European grows close to the ground, more of a runner. American is upright and has smaller leaves and flowers. The flowers are tubular, bluish lilac. The leaves are hairy, toothed with a strong mint odor. American pennyroyal leaves are ½ to 1 inch long, whereas European is about ½ inch long. The best use for Pennyroyal is as an insect repellent. It is not advisable to use internally. Crush leaves and rub on your skin to keep insects away. Can also be used to keep fleas off your pets. American and European start easily from cuttings. Most gardeners start seed in spring or fall. Separate young plants 4 to 6 inches apart. Plants spread easily. Pick sprigs of pennyroyal anytime. In early summer cut off plants several inches above ground and hang to dry, can also use a dehydrator. Store in an air tight container.

CARNATION; as with all flowers only use ones you grow yourself. This is a perennial flower that grows 16 to 18 inches tall. Carnations are sometimes called Pinks. This tall slender flowercomes in white, red or pink. The flower head is fluffy with many petals. The leaves are narrow. Blooms last a long time. They have a spicy clove-like fragrance. Only the petals are edible and have a spicy, peppery, clove taste. They are used in marmalade, candied, pickled with mace and cinnamon, in vinegar, or even minced in stuffing's; and of course for pretty arrangements making the air fragrant, or a lovely buttoner. Carnations are fairly easy to grow. Sow seed in early spring, make sure soil is not to wet. Cover seeds lightly with ¼ inch of fine soil. Space 12 inches apart. They prefer full sun, and rich well drained soil. During dry periods water once or twice a week. Add fertilizer once or twice a month. Perennials should be mulched for winter.

CHRYSANTHEMUM; Again use only ones that you grow. This is a perennial plant that grows 15 inches tall. A bushy plant has divided, aromatic, green leaves. They come in a wide variety of flower colors and shapes, daisy like, button or pom-poms and may bloom for 2 to 3 weeks. They have a tangy taste. The leaves are used in stir fries, salads and for flavoring vinegars. Flower petals are used as a garnish. Grow in well drained soil. Medium sunlight. Needs frequent watering, keep soil evenly moist. Plants may not survive winter.

CORNFLOWER; is an annual that grows 12 to 30 inches tall. This is a bushy plant that has narrow, lance shaped, silvery green leaves. Stems are topped with fluffy flowers, that come in shades of blue, purple, pink or red.Only use what you grow as others may have been sprayed with pesticides. Cornflowers have a sweet to spicy clove like taste. Use only the petals for garnishes. Also for pretty aromatic flower arrangements. Sow seed in early spring or early fall. Plant seed 1/8 inch deep.Cornflowers self sow if you leave a few flowers to set seed. They like full sun, but will tolerate partial shade. Average to well drained soil.

JASMINE; is a perennial shrub or vine. Shrubby or vine climber with small white flowers, blooms almost all year. The delicate sweet flavor, used for teas. Use only what you grow as others may have been sprayed with pesticide. Grow in pots, with rich soil, as a hanging vine. Fertilize twice a month in spring through summer. Needs half a day of direct sun light. Grows best in warm climates. Keep soil very moist.

GERANIUMS; are shrubby or trailing perennials. They can grow to 4 feet tall. Leaves may be round, scalloped, or intricately cut. Some have pleasant scents or multi-colored markings. They flower in spring and summer, although some bloom year round. Flowers come in white, red or bi-colors. Ivy geraniums have trailing stems. Use only plants that you have grown. Sprinkle over deserts and in refreshing drinks or freeze in ice cubes. Scented geraniums are used to scent jellies, linens, sugar, and butter. You can really experiment with these leaves. They need good light with full sun in winter. Allow to dry between waterings. Needs heavy sandy soil in small pots. Repot in spring. Fertilize monthly in spring and summer.

MARIGOLD; is an annual that grows from 6 to 36 inches tall and spreads 6 to 18 inches wide. This is a hardy annual with bright 2 to 4 inch wide flowers and bushy mounds of lacy green leaves. They come in shades of yellow, orange and red. Some types are tall with large flowers, others are smaller with small dainty flowers. Marigold is a wonderful companion plant for tomatoes and veggies. They help to keep bugs away from the veggies, also add a pretty touch to the veggie patch. They also make a very attractive border plant For earliest bloom start seed indoors and transplant after last frost. Can also plant seeds after last frost. They prefer full sun and average well drained soil. Light afternoon shade will help prolong blooming.

PANSY; perennials, usually grown as an annual that grows 6 to 8 inches tall. Plants form tidy oval to narrow green leaves. Flat 5 petaled flowers form just above clumps of leaves. 2 to 5 inches wide flowers bloom in a range of colors, white, pink, red, orange, yellow, purple, blue and near black; often with contrasting faces. Aside from being really beautiful and sweet smelling border plants, their leaves can be used in green and fruit salads. They have a slightly sweet to musky taste. Only use ones you grow in foods. To bloom in same year buy plants in early spring or start seed indoors 8 to 10 weeks before last frost. They like full to partial shade with a moist well drained soil. As with all flowers only use what you have grown.

ROSES; this is a perennial that comes in many types from dwarf to bush and climbers. There are to many to mention in this book, as we are only interested in the culinary uses. Aside from beautiful to look at, and making wonderful arrangements and buttonhole flowers there are other uses. Make sure petals and hips are disease free before using them. Also that they have not been sprayed or dusted recently. NEVER use Rose leaves. Rose Honey is a really sweet. You can also crystallize the petals. Adding petals to a wine vinegar adds a nice taste. Petals can be used in syrups, jellies, perfumed butters and sweet spreads. Crystallized roses on fruit compote is divine. Try rose-sugar on carrots. The white portion of petals is bitter. Plants need shelter from cold winds. A fairly drained soil is what they like. They like full sun. Keep soil moist during summer. Mulch roses for good results. Watch carefully for various diseases and aphids. Buy a good handbook on caring for roses.

SAFFRON CROCUS; is a perennial that grows 1 foot tall in zones 6 to 9. Lavender, white or purplish flowers bloom in fall. They look just like the crocus that bloom in spring except that the flowers have vivid orange yellow stigmas [centers]. They have narrow grass like leaves that grow 6 to 12 inches long. Saffron threads [stigmas] are used in many rice dishes as well as with veggies, meat, poultry dishes and in baked goods. Plant the bulbs [corms] in spring or fall, place root side down, 3 to 4 inches below surface. Lift and divide every 3 to 4 years in early summer. Saffron prefers partial shade but tolerates full sun. Plant in well drained soil. Space bulbs 6 inches apart. Harvest the orange yellow stigmas [centers] in fall when flowers are fully open. Gather in morning, after flowers are fully open, with tweezers pull out the 3 stigmas. Dry them on the fruit leather insert of dehydrator or between sheets of brown paper in an airy space.

SUNFLOWERS; are annuals but self seed and grow 4 to 12 feet tall. The sunflower has a large yellow flower with dark brown to black centers. The common sunflower is usable for oil or snacks of seeds. To roast the seeds put sunflower seeds in a shallow pan in a 300 degree oven for 30 to 40 minutes, or until golden brown, stirring occasionally. Take out of oven and add one teaspoon of melted butter or marg to one cup of seeds. Stir to coat, put on paper towel and salt to taste. Sunflowers need soil with adequate water holding capacity and proper fertility. They need plenty of water for 20 days before and after flowering. Plant seed in moist soil 1 to 2 inches deep, space 12 inches apart, or can be started in 4 inch peat pots and transplant outdoors. Harvest begins in mid September and can run into October. When florets in center are shriveled and head is down turned, cut seed head with about 1 foot of stem and hang to dry. Put cheesecloth over heads to catch seeds as they drop. Can also allow to dry on plant but need to protect from birds by covering heads with cheesecloth.

VIOLET; is a perennial that grows 6 inches tall in zones 5 to 8. Purple, blue, pink or white ½ inch flowers, have 2 upper petals and 3 below. Central bottom petal forms a tube at the base and contains the antlers. Petals are often streaked or striped and bloom in early spring. Leaves are oval, kidney or heart shaped, dark green smooth or downy leaves and reach 2½ inches wide. Fresh leaves are an excellent edible garnish. Add young leaves to salads, only if you grow them yourself. Plant young plants in the garden in spring, summer, or early fall. Prefers full shade but tolerates full sun. Likes moist well drained soil. Mulch each fall with leaves for winter protection. Pick flowers when fully open. Gather young leaves in early spring. Cut each flower or leaf with its stem. To dry press between sheets of absorbent paper in a book

CHAPTER 11

Trees<Shrubs & Vines>

TREES< SHRUBS AND VINES>

Trees are wonderful things. Youngsters can take a book, climb up into their own world to enjoy a good read, and if you're in the right tree there's even a snack right there. What a wonderful place to read, to dream while sitting there, up in the air. A shrub or bush is a neat hiding place, can read in peace or pretend and play hide and seek. As well as this fun side of trees and shrubs they provide so very much for us. Food, shelter, fuel all of this beauty and air too.

APPLE TREE; is a deciduous tree, loses leaves in winter. It grows 8 to 30 feet tall, depending on the type, in zones 3 to 9. Leaf is an alternate oval 2 to 5 inches long and 1¼ to 2½ inches wide, downy on the underside. Flowers white with pink tinge and 5 petals. Fruit appears in fall. Plant full sized trees 25 to 30 feet apart, dwarfs 6 to 8 feet apart, semi-dwarfs 12 to 15 feet apart. Give plenty of moisture and nutrients. Mulch with compost in spring make sure soil is moist around mature trees when they're in bloom. Prune in early spring and continue yearly pruning until trees are mature. Apples will start producing fruit in 2 to 5 years. Apples are good raw, baked, or in jellies and jams, they are also good dried.

APRICOT; grows 8 to 24 feet tall in zones 5 to 9. Leaves are oval 2 to 3½ inches long and 1½ to 3 inches wide with a rounded base and pointed tip. Flowers are 1 to 2 inches around, 5 white to pinkish petals. Plant at least 2 trees, so they can cross pollinate. Plant full sized trees 25 feet apart, dwarf trees ,12 to 15 feet apart. Mulch with compost in spring and fertilize as needed. Should be pruned. Pluck fruits when soft and sweet. Apricots are good fresh or in jams and jellies.

ALMOND; grows 12 to 30 feet tall in zones 6 to 9. Young shoots are green at first, becoming purplish, then gray in second year. Leaves are ½ inch long and ¾ to 1½ inch wide. Flowers are white or pale pink, 1 to 2 inches with 5 petals, singly or pairs before leaves in early spring. Need to plant at least 2 trees to pollinate. Plant 25 feet apart and mulch with compost each spring. Water plants regularly during hot weather. When pruning do more heading than thinning.

BLACKBERRY; is a perennial that grows 4 to 7 feet tall in zones 5 to 9. They need plenty of space as they spread rapidly trailing along the ground. Large compound leaves with 5 to 7 leaflets with white flowers in spring to early summer. Flowers appear in second year. Flowers are ¾ to 1¼ inches. Stems or vines are very thorny. Fruit appears in late summer. The berries are red to almost black. Berries are used fresh, in baking and in jams and jellies, you can also make a good wine. Buy Blackberry as a dry root plant. They need a lot of space. Plant 3 to 4 feet apart. They need good sun exposure and moist soil, compost in early spring. Prune in early spring. Blackberries are ready when entirely black and a little dull. Eat right away or freeze for later.

BLUEBERRY; low or high bush blueberry grow 2 to 15 feet tall in zones 3 to 9. Leaves can be deciduous or evergreen oval from ½ to 3½ inches long and about ½ inch wide. Flowers are bell shaped white, pale pink or red sometimes with a greenish tinge. Plant in full sun in average to rich well drained soil. Depending on the type you are growing, plant 2 to 8 feet apart. Apply a thick layer of mulch to keep soil moist. Add compost every spring. Pinch off all flowers first year to strengthen the bush. Harvest the berries after they turn blue. Don't pick under ripe berries they wont ripen. Blueberries can be eaten fresh or used to make jelly, jams and juices can also be used in baked goods.

BEECHNUT; is a deciduous that grows to 100 feet tall in zones 4 to 8. Leaves are sparsely toothed 2 to 6 inches long and 1½ to 4 inches wide. Small greenish flowers and catkins appear in spring after new leaves appear. The bark is smooth and light gray. Fruit is small, sharp 3 angled nut 4 to 6 inches long, in a soft spined husk. Nuts are edible and in Canada and the U.K. they make syrup from Beech sap. Beech trees like deep, loamy, moist, humus rich, well drained soil. Transplant in spring. Prune when able to establish a straight, upright trunk. Beech has shallow roots so keep well drained.

BANANA; is a tropical plant that grows 20 to 25 feet tall. Fruit grows in hanging clusters a bunch of bananas can be green, yellow or red. The stalk will die and be replaced by another. Leaves are spirally arranged and may grow to 9 feet long and 2 feet wide. Banana is actually a plant and not a tree. A single flower is produced by each stem [male]. The flowers [female] that produce fruit grow further up the stem. Leaves are a shiny dark green. Stalks are brown.

CHERRY; grows 15 to 30 feet tall in zones 4 to 9. Sweet cherries, need to have two for cross pollination. Sour cherries are self fertile, so you can harvest from just one tree. Space regular sweet cherry trees 20 to 30 feet apart, sour cherries 20 feet apart,and dwarf cherries 10 feet apart. Mulch with compost in early spring. In cooler climates, plant with a northern exposure away from valleys to protect flowers from frost. Cherries begin to bear fruit 3 to 7 years after planting . If weather is dry let cherries ripen on trees for best flavor. Flowers in spring. Known for their beautiful blossoms, white or pink. Blossoms, generally, have 5 petals. New leaves don't appear till after the flowers. Most leaves are green to copper brown.

CHESTNUT; grows 40 feet or more in zones5 to 9. Plant in full sun in average to rich, well drained soil. You need two trees for better crops. Plant 40 to 80 feet apart. Mulch to eliminate weeds, apply compost or fertilizer in late spring after last frost. Chestnuts bear in 3 to 5 years. In fall nuts mature and drop to ground. Pick them up promptly. Leaf has toothed edge. Elongated oval in shape. The edge of each tooth is bristled and dark green in color. The bur is a dense mass of long slender spines. Spines are about 1 inch long, each bur has up to 3 nuts.

CITRUS; [orange, lemon, grapefruit etc.] grows 10 to 30 feet tall in zones 8 to 10. Frost will damage the fruit of any citrus plants and sometimes the rest of the tree. Plant them in full sun to light shade in average to rich well drained soil. Citrus trees area nearly all self fertile, so you only need one to get a harvest. Space large citrus trees 25 feet apart and dwarf trees 10 feet apart. Paint the trunks with white latex paint to prevent sunburn. Keep soil moist to prevent early fruit drop. Mulch well and fertilize as needed. Most citrus trees produce fruit 3 or 4 years after planting. Citrus trees have spiny shoots and alternate evergreen leaves. Single flowers with white petals and numerous stamens. They have a very strong scent [a heavenly aroma]. The fruit has leathery skin. The actual fruit is loaded with Vitamin C.

COCONUT; is a member of the palm family and grows to 30 feet tall in tropical climates. Leaves are pinnate and grow up to 6 feet long. The trunk is smooth. Coconut needs sandy soil, prefers abundant sunlight. They need high humidity for best growth. Intolerant of cold. The nut, when young, is green and later turns brown. This tree needs a tropical climate.

CRANBERRY; grows in zones 2 to 6. It grows 1 foot tall but spread is unlimited. Cranberries thrive in the sun and moist, well drained, humus rich soil. The plants do not tolerate dry soil, but can withstand flooding in cold weather. Plant in spring or fall where winters are mild, or in spring where winters are severe. Space plants 1 to 2 feet apart. Mix plenty of acid peat into soil before planting. Mix with sawdust or sand; renew mulch periodically. Pick berries in fall after they are fully colored. Cranberries will keep for 2 to 4 months at high humidity and temps just above freezing. Cranberry is an evergreen shrub with slender wiry stems. The flowers are dark pink. The fruit is a false berry that is larger than the plants leaves, it starts out white and deep red when fully ripe.

CURRANT and GOOSEBERRY; grow 3 to 7 feet tall in zones 3 to 7. Plant 2 or more plants for a better harvest. Plant in full sunlight to light shade in average soil. Space plants 6 feet apart and mulch well. Add compost in early spring and water regularly in dry weather. Prune in winter remove all shoots over 3 years old. For cooking or making jelly, pick currants and gooseberries when they are not quite ripe. For eating fresh let them ripen. Gooseberry canes produce a spine at each leaf node and bear grape size berries. Currant canes lack spines or prickles and bear 8 to 30 smaller fruit in clusters.

DATE TREE; grows best in desert locals. It grows 45 to 75 feet tall. The date tree often has several trunks from a single root. Leaves are pinnate 9 to 15 feet long with spines. Fruit is 1¼ to 2 ¾ inches long and ¾ to 1¼ inches around; when unripe they range from bright red to yellow in color. They are easily grown from seed, but only 50 percent of seedlings will bear fruit. Plants grown from cuttings will fruit 2 to 3 years earlier than seedling plants. Date palms can take 4 to 7 years after planting to bear fruit.

FIG TREE; grows in tropical climates, also in rain forests, zone 8 to 10. Needs full sun and average well drained soil. It grows 10 to 25 feet tall. Buy a self pollinating type. Space 25 feet apart. Mulch with compost as needed. Fig Trees produce their first crop a year after planting. Ripe figs are soft, with a slightly flexible neck. Keep in fridge for a few days or cut and dry them.

AVACADO TREE; grows 65 feet tall with alternate leaves 4¾ to 9¾ inches long. Flowers are inconspicuous, greenish-yellow, ¼ to ½ inches wide. Pear shaped fruit is 2¾ to 8 inches long and has a large central seed. Needs a climate without frost and very little wind. Trees need well aerated soil. The fruit mature on the tree but ripens off the tree. Grows well in California.

GRAPE; grows 4 to 6 feet high and spreads 8 to 15 feet wide in zones 4 to 10. Plant in full sun in average to rich soil. Get 1 year old plants. Before planting set up a support system for vines to cling to. Let vine grow untrained for 1 year, this develops strong roots. Pinch off flowers that year. Keep soil moist and mulch often.

KIWI; is a vine that grows 4 to 6 feet tall and spreads 15 feet in zones 7 to 9. Plant in full sun to light shade in average to poor well drained soil. Plant 40 feet or closer for pollinating. Keep soil moist up to harvest time. Water less as winter approaches. Mulch well, but fertilize lightly if at all. Train vines on post and wire trellis and train vines up a stake. Pick Kiwi fruit in fall, when seeds are black and fruit is firm. Peel before eating.

MULBERRY; grows in zones 5 to 10. Grows to 15 to 30 feet tall. Plant in full sun in aveerage to well drained soil. Plant in spring or fall while plant is dormant. Space plants 10 to 30 feet apart. Harvesting in quantity spread a clean sheet under tree and shake branches. Ripe fruit does not keep well but can be dried.

PEACH and NECTARINE; grows 8 to 15 feet tall in zones 5 to 9. Plant in full sun in average to well drained soil. Most peaches and nectarines are self pollinating so you only need 1 tree. Fertilize in early spring and when fruit first forms. Spray leaves with liquid kelp every 3 to 4 weeks during season. Peach and Nectarine trees produce fruit 2 to 4 years after planting. Harvest when fruit is fully colored. Growing near a wall provides extra warmth for tree.

PEAR; grows 8 to 20 feet tall in zones 4 to 9. Need at least 2 trees for cross pollination. Plant in full sun in average to poor, well drained soil. Space trees 15 to 20 feet apart, dwarfs 8 to 12 feet apart. Mulch with compost in spring. Water as necessary to keep soil moist. Heavy bearing trees need fruit thinning. In June remove smaller fruit, leaving 1 or 2 per cluster. Pear trees generally produce fruit3 to 5 years after planting.

PLUM; grows 8 to 20 feet tall in zones 4 to 10. Plant in full sun in average to rich soil. Most plums self pollinate so only 1 tree is needed. You may get more fruit if you plant 2. Plant 20 to 25 feet apart, dwarfs plant 8 to 12 feet apart. Mulch with compost in spring and keep soil moist through growing season. Apply a complete fertilizer when petals fall. Plum trees generally produce fruit 3 to 4 years after planting. Pick when fruit is soft and sweet.

Chapter 12

Veggies.

VEGGIES.

Purple carrots, blue potatoes, striped tomatoes – what's all that? Yes they're veggies, or so I've heard. Well we're really supposed to eat lots of veggies, so maybe this is Mother Natures way to encourage us to try 'new' things? Don't think I could eat a purple carrot, just wouldn't be right. I've got it, it's natures way of using reverse psychology. Anyhow, veggies are ever so good for us, even if they look funny.

ARTICHOKE; is a perennial that grows 5 feet or more tall in zones 8 to 11. Start seed indoors in late winter. Transplant outdoors in late spring. Seeds are good for 5 years. Plant seeds ¼ inch deep, they will germinate in 10 to 14 days. They need 8 hours of light per day. When transplanting space them 24 inches apart. Water frequently. Allow 3 feet between rows of Artichokes. Be generous with manure and mulch between rows. May produce edible flowers the first year but more likely not to yield a harvest till the second year. Harvest buds in cool, moist weather for best flavor. The bud should be firm, tight and an even green in color. Cut the bud with 1 inch of stem. Rich well drained soil is what an Artichoke prefers, in full sun. It is the tender heart of the prickly vegetable that is used for our eating enjoyment.

ASPARAGAS; is a perennial that grows in zones 3 and warmer. Spears grow 6 to 8 inches tall. Let smaller ones develop into ferns to feed the plant. Seeds are good for3 years. Sow indoors 8 weeks before last frost. Sow seeds ¼ to ½ inch deep. Seeds germinate in 10 to 12 days. Transplant outdoors, in spring, 3 weeks before last frost.

Space plants 18 inches apart. Choose your site well as Asparagus beds are productive for 15 to 20 years. Put in northern part of garden. Seeds need 8 hours of light per day. Make regular applications of compost or manure through the growing season. You can harvest Asparagus in the second spring after planting, third year if you start from seed. Keep well weeded. When harvesting make sure tips are firm. Stop harvesting when most of spears are small and tips are loose.

BUSH BEANS; Types: green, wax, Italian flat pod, French filet, purple types, shell beans, lima beans and fava beans. Where ever you live bush beans will grow easily in your garden. A good companion to the bush bean is the marigold, it helps keep the plant bug free. For bush beans sow seeds 1 inch deep and 3 inches apart, after danger of frost is past. Keep well watered and weeded. Water really well when in flower. To assure steady crops, make several small plantings 3 to 4 weeks apart, ending 2 months before fall frost. Pick before seeds begin to swell. Plant in full sun. Will germinate in 7 to 10 days. Pole beans: Plant 4 plants per hill 15 inches apart. Seeds are good for 3 years. Snap beans- green beans eaten with pod and seeds when young and tender, must be picked at proper time. If left unpicked the plant will stop producing. Green and wax beans should be picked when pod is ¼ to 3/8 inches around, about as big around as a pencil. French or filet beans should be harvested when they are very slender, about 1/8 inch around. Allowed to get larger and they get tough and stringy. Harvest dry beans when pods are completely mature and dry. Air circulation is important so pods don't rot before drying, allow space between rows. If you have rainy weather after the leaves dry pull the plants and hang by the roots to dry indoors. Beans are good to eat after sprouting. Take Pinto beans, and after soaking them for a couple of days, add onions, some meat and chili powder and tomatoes makes a great winters dinner. Add a little grated cheese, after cooking and that is really great.

BEETS; is a root veggie that grows in zone 8 and warmer. Sow 3 to 4 weeks before last frost. For best yield plant in full sun. Beets grow best in cool conditions and profit from cooling mulches. Watering is important. Don't let the soil dry out. Plant 1 inch deep and 2 to 4 inches apart. Thin young plants when 2 to 3 inches tall. Best grown in stone free soil. Beets mature in 55 to 70 days. The greens can also be eaten. Harvest them when large enough to use, but leave at least 1 inch of stem to prevent bleeding. The root, the beet, should be 1 ½ to 2 ½ inches around when harvested. This is my favorite nosh, pickled beets with a slice of cheese um um good.

BROCCOLI; grows in zones 3 and warmer. This is a winter veggie. Sow outdoors in early summer for a fall crop. Sow seeds ¼ inch deep in full sun. Space beds 16 inches apart. Needs moderate watering. Will have sprouts in 4 to 7 days. Mulch to keep soil evenly moist. Should be ready to harvest in 70 to 95 days. Harvest before flower buds turn yellow. Fertilize Broccoli every 3 to 4 weeks with an organic fertilizer. For best harvest the head should be dark green and the buds should be tight. To save blanche and freeze. Broccoli cheese soup is a really good winter treat.

BRUSSEL SPROUTS; is a winter veggie that grows in zones 4 to 7. Sow indoors 4 to 6 weeks before last frost, or outdoors in early summer for fall crop. Sow seeds ¼ inch deep. Seeds should sprout in 5 to 8 days. Space, outdoors, 16 to 18 inches apart. Seeds are good for 4 years. Brussel Sprouts do best in evenly moist soil. Apply mulch, such as straw, during warm months. Keep a layer of compost under the mulch. Plants grow up to 3 feet tall so stake when small so as not to harm roots. Fertilize every 3 to 4 weeks. Brussel Sprouts like full sun. They are a hardy veg and continue to do well even in snow. Harvest lower sprouts first, anytime until early winter. Finish harvesting before ground freezes. Harvested sprouts freeze well. For me I could make a meal of this delishish veggie.

CABBAGE; grows in zones 3 and warmer. Needs well drained rich soil. Can be grown as a spring and fall crop. Sow indoors, for spring crop, 4 to 6 weeks before last frost. For fall crop plant outdoors 10 to 12 weeks before first frost. Plant seeds ¼ inch deep, they will sprout in 5 days. Space 12 to 18 inches apart. Cabbage likes full sun. Seeds last for 4 years. Keep Cabbage well mulched and weed free. Cabbage should mature in 60 to 110 days. Early Cabbage does not store well. When they are the size of a softball they are most tender, ready for use. Maybe corned beef and cabbage for dinner. Late cabbage stores well. Leave roots on and lean against root cellar wall. Cabbage patch stew and cole slaw for winter goodies. Stuffed cabbage leaves are good too. Cabbage is easy to grow and an excellent source of vitamin C. Be careful not to over water as the heads will split.

CARROTS; grow in zones 3 and warmer. Carrots like deep, light soil in full sun. Sow first crop in early spring. Seeds are very small. Plant only ½ inch deep and firm the seed bed gently with the back of your hoe. Seeds sprout in 6 days. Thin to 2 to 3 inches apart. Plant more crops every few weeks till 3 months before first frost. Do not over water as it can cause root rot. Carrots should be ready to eat in 50 to 70 days. Pull when ground is moist, or dig with a garden fork. Because carrot seeds are so tiny they have a hard time breaking through the soil.. Help them out by planting radishes with them. The radishes will creak through first and loosen the soil for the carrots. Who found out that bunnies have good eyesight?? As a child I was told they did, to encourage me to eat them. They didn't need to encourage me as carrots are yummy cooked or raw.

CAULIFLOWER; grows in zones 3 and warmer. Sow seeds ¼ to ½ inch deep in rich well drained soil in full sun. Can be started indoors. They sprout in 6 days. Do not put indoor plants outside to early, after frost is best, as frost may cause the Cauliflower to stop growing. Start fall crops 90 to 120 days before fall frost, set out seedlings when 4 to 5 weeks old. Keep well watered and give compost tea. When heads appear, use a clothes pin to clip several large leaves together over the head to shade it and keep it white or remove a large lower leaf and lay it over the top of the developing head. Cauliflowers matures in 50 to 72 days. You should be able to harvest about 4 days after tying the leaves .The head should be tight and not beginning to curl. Cauliflower now comes in orange, purple and green as well as white. Seeds are good for 4 years.

CELERY; grows in zones 5 and warmer. Start seed indoors 4 to 6 weeks before last frost. Celery is a slow starter. Should sprout in about 7 days. Celery likes soil that holds the water and is in full sun. Work manure into the soil. Set plants 10 to 12 inches apart. Do not let the soil dry out. Plant should be mature in 80 to 105 days. To harvest cut at soil line when plant is the size you want. Seeds are good for 3 years.

CELERIAC; A relative of celery. Grows in zones 5 and up. Needs soil the same as celery and in full sun. This plant is grown for its root and not for the stalk. Start indoors 6 to 8 weeks before last spring frost and set out 10 to 12 inches apart when threat of frost is over. Keep bed well weeded and watered. Apply compost tea at least monthly. Should mature in 110 to 120 days. To harvest loosen soil around the plant with a garden fork and lift the plant free. Cut the tops 1 to 2 inches above the root and store as you would any root veggie.

SWEET CORN; grows in zones 3 and warmer. Do not start indoors. Sow after last spring frost. Sow seeds 1 inch deep in well manured soil, in full sun. Corn should sprout in 4 days after planting. Corn grows rapidly and needs adequate watering. Apply fish emulsion or compost tea after 1 month and again when tassels appear. Water is most critical when tassels appear. The time to pick is when the corn has a small amount of pliant greenish silk near the top of the husk, with dry, brownish silk at the ends. Pick corn early in the morning and refrigerate till ready to use.

CUCUMBER; grows in zones 4 and warmer. Cucumbers are climbers and will save a lot of space if you provide them with some kind of trellis. They like full sun and don't do well with frost either at the beginning or end of their growing season. Fertilize with fish emulsion every 2 weeks. when flowers appear it is important to keep even soil moisture. Sow 3 seeds to each pot, indoors, ½ to 1 inch deep, 3 to 4 weeks before you want to plant outdoors. Transplant after danger of frost is past. Seeds sprout in 3 to 4 days. Seeds are good for 5 years. You can harvest when large enough for your use. Harvest when fruit is still dark green all over. Best eaten fresh. Should mature in 48 to 70 days.

EGGPLANT; grows in zones 5 and warmer. It is not recommended to start outdoors. Plant seed indoors, ¼ inch deep 4 to 6 weeks before last frost. Eggplant likes very sunny weather, so don't set plants out to soon. Eggplants like well drained soil with plenty of moisture. Use fish emulsion or compost tea at least once a month. Space plants 18 inches apart. Harvest plants after they've reached half their mature size. Early harvested plants are more tender. Cut fruits from plants with shears leaving some stem attached. Eat soon as Eggplant doesn't store well. Seed should sprout in 7 days.

ENDIVE and ESCAROLE; grows in zones 4 and warmer. These are really varieties of the same plant, with slightly different tastes. Endive has curly or crinkly edged leaves and a sharp some what bitter taste. Escarole is hardier with flat, some what thicker leaves and a less bitter flavor. Sow seeds ¼ inch deep indoors 8 weeks before last frost. Plant out doors after chance of frost is over. Space plants 12 inches apart. Plant in full sun, in fertile well drained soil. Should mature in 80 to 100 days. Cut the entire head at the base in the morning. Seeds are good for 4 to 6 years.

GARLIC; grows in zones 5 to 10. Plant individual cloves in October for harvesting next summer. Plant 2 inches deep and 6 inches apart. Garlic prefers full sun, needs humus rich well drained soil. Give compost in early spring. Will grow up to 2 feet tall. Interplant lettuce or beets to keep the soil cool during summer. When flower buds appear cut them back to encourage larger bulbs. Harvest Garlic in late summer when the bottom 2 leaves have turned yellow, or the tops fall off. Loosen the soil with a garden fork and pull the bulbs. Spread the bulbs on a screen for good air circulation and cure in full sun. Can also hang plants from ceiling in a cool, humid dark place.

KALE; is a very sturdy veggie. Even grows in the snow. Sow in doors 6 weeks before last frost. Out doors, in cool climates, late spring or early summer, in warm climates early spring and for over wintering late summer or early fall. Sow seeds ½ inch deep. Should sprout in 5 to 7 days. Space plants 16 inches apart. Does best in full sun but needs cool moist soil, so be sure to keep well watered through the growing season, stop watering after first frost. Fertilize every 2 to 3 weeks. Kale is a very easy to grow veggie and has a very high vitamin and mineral content. Harvest as soon as leaves are big enough to toss in a salad. Use scissors or a knife to gather leaves, try to avoid cutting the stem. Leaves will store for 2 weeks to a month if in a veggie storage bag in the fridge.

KOHLRABI; This is a fall or winter veggie. Kohlrabi, to be tender, needs to grow fast. Sow out doors: In cool climates from 1 month before last frost for spring crops, and early summer for fall crops. In warmer climates, in late winter for spring crops and fall for early winter crops. Sow seeds ¼ to ½ inches deep, space 6 to 8 inches apart. Best in full sun, water evenly. Fertilize every 2 to 3 weeks. As stems begin to swell add a layer of compost or well rotted manure. Harvesting for fresh use begin when stems are about 2 inches around. Pull the entire plant and trim off the leaves and roots. Store plants in fridge, they will keep for a month or two. For winter storage harvest 3 to 4 inch stems after a few frosts. Trim leaves and store in root cellar. Zone 6 and farther south, Kohlrabi can stay in the garden and be harvested as needed. If a cold snap is forecasted mulch plants with straw.

LEEKS; grow in zones3 and warmer. Start Leeks in doors in late winter. Sow in flats ¼ inch deep. They will germinate in 5 to 7 days. Transplant out doors when about 2 inches tall. Fertilize every 2 weeks. Space 6 inches apart. Likes full sun but will tolerate partial shade. Don't transplant till a week after last frost. Leeks grow best with a lot of compost. Water regularly through out growing season. Leeks will stay fresh all winter long under a thick blanket of mulch. Harvest from late summer through winter. Loosen soil gently with a garden fork and pull plants. Leeks don't store well, about a week in fridge, so harvest only what you need. Leeks are a delicious veggie For a winter treat Leek and Potato soup is really great.

LETTUCE; grows in all zones. Grow as a winter veggie in mild climates. Full sun in cool weather, partial shade in warm. Needs a fertile well drained soil. Leaf lettuce is the quickest and easiest to grow. Head lettuce takes longer and needs more space. Direct seed leafy types a month before last frost. Sow ¼ to ½ inch deep. Sow when soil can be worked. Seeds should sprout in 7 to 14 days. Leaf lettuce doesn't need spacing. Head lettuce should be spaced 8 to 12 inches apart. Moderate watering. To encourage fast growth, add plenty of finished compost before planting and again, on the side, a week or so after seedlings appear. Give feedings of compost tea every few weeks until harvest it takes about a month for lettuce to be salad ready. Cut leaf lettuce about 1 inch above ground, that way you'll get a second harvest. Harvest head lettuce as they develop to the size you want.

OKRA; grows in zones 5 and warmer. In cooler climates grow it indoors 5 weeks before last frost. Warmer climates sow out doors after last frost. Sow in full sun putting seeds ¾ inch deep. Space 12 to 15 inches apart. Needs food and water. Irrigate during hot weather. Fertilize once a month. Use a natural fertilizer such as fish emulsion or seaweed. Matures in 50 to 60 days. Clip or pinch off pods when they are 1 to 4 inches long and still soft. Harvest daily in warm weather. Freezes well.

ONION: grows in zone 3 and warmer. Sow seeds indoors 2 months before last frost. Sow seeds ½ inch deep. Can sow outdoors in spring. Onions should sprout in 4 to 5 days after sowing. Space plants 3 to 4 inches apart. Plant in full sun. Onions like a loose, sandy loam with plenty of compost or well rotted manure worked in to the soil before planting. Onions have a shallow root system. They don't like a lot of water but need to be watered regularly. Mulch to maintain soil moisture. Bulb Onions should mature in 60 to 115 days. For immediate use pull as needed. For storage, wait until tops have fallen over and pull 2 days later. Let dry in a cool place. Not all onions store well. Walla

Walla should be used within a few weeks of harvesting and others keep well for months.

PARSNIPS: are cousins of carrots. They take longer to mature. Plant, out doors, ½ inch deep in rows 4 to 6 inches apart. Keep the soil evenly moist during germination period. Parsnips should sprout in 12 to 14 days. When they are 4 to 6 inches high thin them to 3 to 4 inches apart. Put a layer of leaf mold around the plants and mulch with straw. You're now done till next spring. You can harvest Parsnips at the end of growing season, although for best flavor they need to go through a hard winter. A wonderful spring treat is Parsnips sliced thinly and sautéed in butter, over a low flame, till tender.

PEAS: grow in zones 2 and warmer, There are a variety of Peas, but they come in two types bush and pole. Pole peas need a trellis. They can be grown as spring and fall crops. Sow out doors as soon as soil can be worked. In late summer for a fall crop. Plant seeds 1 inch deep and 1 inch apart. Best in full sun but will tolerate partial shade. Seeds should sprout in 14 days. In preparing soil for Peas dig in plenty of manure in the fall, making ground is ready for spring planting. Peas like a loose well drained soil. Peas do not do well in hot weather, so plant early for spring crops. Make sure to water well when they are in bloom. Peas should be mature in 55 to 80 days. Peas are really sweet if you pick them at the right time; otherwise, they turn starchy. Pick Snow Peas as soon as pod reaches mature length and before the peas are fully developed. The just right stage doesn't last more than a day or two so check often. Sugar Peas are best when pod and peas are plump. Pick Garden peas when pods have filled out but aren't bulging around the peas. Pods left to long on the vine signal the plant to stop producing. Magic Peas! Magic that there were any left to cook. As a child my job was to shell them. They are ever so good eaten raw. So do enjoy Magic Peas, which ever kind you like to eat.

PEPPERS. BELL PEPPERS; grow in zones 4 and warmer. Peppers come in a variety of colors and shapes but all are grown the same way. They need to be started in doors. Plant ¼ inch deep 8 weeks before last frost. If buds form, before transplanting, nip them off as roots aren't strong enough to support them. Transplant out doors after any danger of frost is over. Space plants 12 inches apart in full sun. Keep the soil evenly moist. You can harvest Peppers when they are green most are completely ripe when red. When you harvest is a personal choice. Red Peppers are sweeter than green, so harvesting Bell Peppers is a matter of personal choice.

POTATOES; grow in zones 3 and warmer. Potatoes come in many colors red, yellow, blue and gold, and varieties. Time your planting according to where you live. Warm climate, in fall. Warm temperate areas, late winter. Cool climate, early to mid spring. Starting with seed potatoes. Some seed potatoes are larger than others. You can plant golf ball size directly in the ground. Large ones need to be cut in to sections. What ever size seed potatoes need some preparation about 2 days before planting. Cut large ones in to pieces about 1 ½ inches thick. Make sure each one has at least 2 eyes. Eyes should be just beginning to sprout, but not having a stem starting to form. Set aside to let them heal for 1 or 2 days. Then treat with a light dusting of agricultural sulphur. Will guard against fungal disease and potato beetles. Before planting work compost not manure in to the soil. Plant 3 to 4 inches deep, 3 weeks before last frost. Space them 12 inches apart. Full sun is best. Water moderately until blossoms appear. Keep plants well watered after blossoms until 2 weeks before harvesting. You can harvest new potatoes a couple of months after planting, either pull plant or feel ground and take a few from each plant leaving rest to mature. Harvest main crop when leaves die, with a garden fork loosen soil. Easiest if you let the soil dry after loosening then harvest the potatoes. Don't wash dirt off, let dry and dust dirt off and store. Do not store with apples.

PUMPKIN; Just for fun. Not really a veggie. Grows in zones 4 and warmer. Sow in doors 3 to 4 weeks before last frost, or sow out doors after last spring frost. Sow seeds ½ to 1 inch deep in soil that you have worked in compost or well rotted manure. Seeds sprout in 6 to 10 days. Pumpkins like full sun and keep them well watered. Mulch until plant begins to vine. Pumpkins are mature in 100 to 115 days. Pumpkins should be a bright orange when ready to harvest. Store in a dry cool place. While pumpkins are still small and skin is soft, scratch a childs name on one. The name will stay and grow along with the pumpkin. It's a nice surprise for the child at harvest time.

RADICCHIO; Grows in all but the coldest climate. Sow seeds ¼ inches deep in doors 8 weeks before last frost or out doors 2 weeks before last frost and 2 months before first fall frost. Radicchio tolerates cold and frost very well so is a great winter veggie. Plants should be spaced 8 to 10 inches apart. Radicchio likes full sun. Harvest as soon as heads are firm. This veggie has a zippy flavor, nice to add to salads.

RADISHES; grow in all zones. Sow out doors. In cool climates early spring and fall; in warm climates, winter. Sow seeds ½ inch deep. Radishes like ground that has had leaves worked in to the soil. Space plants 2 inches apart. Best yields in full sun with heavy watering. Seeds should sprout in 4 to 12 days. They mature in 21 to 35 days for spring radishes; 50 to 60 days for winter radishes. Pull spring and fall crops when big enough to eat. Harvest all roots before hard frost. Store in damp sand.

RHUTABAGA; grows in zone 3 and warmer. Best planted out doors. Work compost or leaf mold in to soil before sowing. Sow seeds ½ inch deep in early summer or, in cool regions, mid summer. Seeds should sprout in 3 to 5 days. Space plants 8 inches apart. Rhutabagas do best in full sun with moderate watering. Should mature in 90 to 110 days. Will with stand severe frost. Pull Rhutabagas when large enough for use. The greens are also edible. Harvest all roots before hard freeze and store in damp sand or sawdust in a cool place.

SPINACH; Grows in all zones. Grows best in the beginning and end of growing season. Grows best in rich organic soil, so work compost in before sowing. Sow seeds ½ inch deep in early spring or in doors 3 to 4 weeks before last frost. Seeds should sprout in 7 to 14 days. Spinach likes full sun or partial shade. Thin 4 to 6 inches apart. Spinach matures in 40 to 53 days. Pick larger outside leaves or harvest whole plant. Cut entire plant 1 inch above soil level, this will encourage plant to grow another crop of leaves. Spinach freezes well for use as a cooked veggie.

SQUASH; grows in zones 3 and warmer. There are a variety of squash but all need the same kind of care for growth. The soil needs to have a lot of compost worked in to it. You can sow seeds ½ to 1 inch deep in doors 3 to 4 weeks before last frost or , out doors when all chance of frost is over. Squash likes full sun, and needs heavy watering. Plant matures in 42 to 65 frost free days. Pick squash small for best flavor. Pick blossoms in early morning before pollination. All summer squash keeps in fridge for about 2 weeks and freezes well.

SWEET POTATOES; grow in zones 5 and warmer. Sweet Potatoes like loose, well drained soil that is not to rich. You need rooting potatoes. To make sweet potato slips, purchase large, firm sweet potatoes about 30 to 40 days before last frost. Either set potatoes in sand in a warm, sunny room or cut in to sections and place each section in a glass of water. Shoots will then rise from the cut section. When shoots are 4 to 6 inches long, gently twist them from the section of potato. Collect shoots and place in water so that only the bottom half is immersed. Slips are ready to plant when roots appear. Don't allow roots to get longer than 1 inch. Plant slips out doors 2 weeks after last frost. Space 14 to 18 inches apart. Sweet Potatoes like full sun and low watering, except when first planted they need lots of water. Dig Sweet potatoes before frost or as soon as the vines have been killed by a light frost. They store well in a root cellar or similar environment, cool and humid.

TOMATO; grows in zones 3 and warmer. Needs a fertile well drained soil in full sun. Sow in doors 6 to 7 weeks before last frost. Seeds will sprout in6 to 8 days. After all frost is past set out doors 15 inches apart if supported, 24 to 36 inches apart if supported. Buying plants, set out after all frost is past. Water moderate to high during growth, low during harvest. When in full blossom fertilize with weak compost tea or fish emulsion. Tomatoes should mature in 52 to 90 days, frost free days. Pick fruit when evenly colored but firm. Can freeze, dry or can excess fruit. Have a companion plant of Marigold , 'twill keep bugs away.

TURNIP; Grows in all zones. Grow as a winter veggie in mild climates. Turnips need deep, loose soil with lots of organic matter. They don't usually need extra fertilizing. They like full sun. Turnips like cool weather. Sow ½ inch deep ,4 to 6 weeks before last frost, out doors. Thin to 3 inches apart. Use thinned greens fresh or cooked. Water regularly for fast growth in spring. Sow fall crop 8 to 10 weeks before first frost. Turnips mature in 35 to 60 days, they will withstand light frost. Harvest Turnips, roots, when they are 1 to 3 inches around. Bigger ones are not so tasty. Can store in fridge for a short time, best eaten fresh. Peas make a good companion plant, some say the peas help turnips grow.

WATERMELON; Just for fun! Grows in all zones. Start in doors 3 weeks before last frost. Sow seeds ½ inch deep. Seed sprouts in 3 to 5 days. Transplant out doors spacing 16 inches apart. Watermelon needs full sun. Their soil should have plenty of compost and some seaweed or rotted manure. Watermelons are sensitive to drought so keep well watered. When harvesting a watermelon, rap it lightly. You should hear a low-pitched "thunk" or "thump." You don't want to hear a 'ping'. The tendril nearest the fruit turns from green to brown. The underside of the melon, where it sits on the ground, is yellow. No worry on how to store, that doesn't happen they are far to tasty to last that long.